Tony Pearson was crowned 1978 Mr. America at the height of the Golden Age of Bodybuilding; that span of years that transformed American bodybuilding from a subculture into a mainstream activity. I'm proud to have known Tony for more than four decades, from the moment a teenaged Tony walked into the first and only Gold's Gym in California, fresh off a one-way ticketed, cross-country bus ride from his St. Louis home. When you think of the Golden Age of Bodybuilding and Gold's Gym, Tony Pearson stands out. Neither the sport nor the gym would be as popular today were it not for the impact of Tony Pearson. Tony's story is a remarkably inspiring tale of success, a young man who triumphed over much adversity to reach the top of his chosen sport.

Ken Sprague
Owner of the first Gold's Gym, 1972-1979

GW00646474

DRIVEN

My Secret Story

Tony Pearson

ISBN2 978-0-578-51704-9

Permission to use material from other works

COVER: Annette Wood

IMAGES: Courtesy of AP Associated Press, Shawn Ray, Bob Gruskin, Chiqullin Garcia. Michael Neveux

Printed in the United States of America

drivenbytonypearson@gmail.com

To my Mother, thank you for being the strongest, bravest Mom I could ever hope for. Your unconditional love, advice, wisdom and understanding is unequalled. I am truly blessed and honored to have you as my Mom. Love, Tony

CONTENTS

ACKNOWLEDGEMENTS

My sincere thanks to Arnold Schwarzenegger for inspiring me on that fateful day at muscle beach. And for the encouragement to believe in myself and to follow my dream.

Special thanks to my dear friends Steve and Deana Campbell for their amazing generosity, love and support throughout the whole process of completing this project.

I'm extremely grateful to my friends Martha McCue and Sal DeFilippo for their guidance in putting the final touches on the long and challenging journey completing this book.

To my friend and coach Glenn Hall. Words couldn't fully convey my appreciation to you for restoring my health and giving me the opportunity to continue living a fitness lifestyle.

A warm appreciation for the unerring support from my friends and colleagues that believed in me and cheered me on to finish the story.

PROLOGUE

I was ten years old. Bent over picking cotton on a blistering, hot day in the fields of Mississippi with my great-Auntie Bettie Pearson, I suddenly stopped and stood up. The sweat was still pouring down my face, but I took no notice. I heard a crowd chanting my name. Tony! Tony! Tony! I looked around. Where did they come from? Who was saying my name so loudly? All the pickers were still intent on picking, as they had been all morning. No one was turned my way or looking at me. Was I the only one who heard my name shouted out with, it seemed, great enthusiasm?

Whap! Whap! The violent blow to the back of my head sent me reeling to the ground. I fell on top of the huge sack I'd been filling with cotton balls. The crowd sound faded away and I came back to reality with my Auntie Bettie screaming at me, preparing to hit me again.

"Boy! Why didya stop pickin'? Have ya lost yer damn mind? Git yer ass back down der an' pick dat cotton. An' don' ya stop til I tellya. Do ya hea me, boy?"

"Yes, ma'am," I replied with tears running down my face.

As I trembled with fear. I knew that when we got home to Auntie Bettie's shack in the boondocks, I'd get not just my usual beating but an extra harsh one for those few moments when I paused in picking to listen to my name being called out with such tremendous acclaim. Was I dreaming?

CHAPTER 1

"**N**o! Oh! No! Sorry! Sorry, Auntie!"

It was late in the morning at my great-Auntie Bettie's two-room shack. She was standing at the old iron wood-burning stove making breakfast, humming one of her favorite Gospel hymns by Mahalia Jackson, singing, "Precious Lord Take My Hand."

The stove was extremely hot, giving off lots of heat. Every time I passed by it I stopped to feel its warmth because in the other room, where I slept, I was always too cold. I was being a normal three-year-old, playing with my ball that I brought with me from my mom and dad's house. I ran and stumbled through the shack making a lot of noise. I was a rambunctious kid like most my age. At my mom and dad's house, I could play as hard as I wanted as long as I wasn't bothering anyone.

"Go sit down an' stop dat runnin'," Auntie Bettie Ansaid calmly.

"No!" I replied.

"I said, go sit down."

"No!" I repeated.

She grabbed hold of me, her grip tightening as she swung

me back and forth and lifted me in the air. Then she pulled back the top of the stove to one side, exposing flames that leapt up high. She held me over the fire. I was screaming until my three-year-old vocal cords almost gave out. I squirmed and twisted in Auntie's strong, calloused hands as she dangled me by both arms and a leg over the flames of the stove. Twice she lowered me closer to the fiery heat that was licking at my bare feet and arms. The pain was unbearable. I continued to scream. For a moment my back touched the red hot chimney pipe that went through the roof and I cried out in agony. I was terrified she'd let go and drop me into the burning furnace.

"I'll' teach ya ta mind me!" she yelled, still holding me over the flames. "I'll burn yer lil' black ass alive if ya don' listen ta me. Ya never say no ta me, do ya hea' me, boy?"

My tears and fright made my voice quiver. I can still hear the way I croaked out, "Yes, ma'am," in my desperate plea. Finally, she swung me down to the floor. I wobbled over to crouch in a dark corner, the farthest away from her as I could find. I tried to sob quietly in order not to get her upset again. My skin was red and starting to blister, the pain sharp and searing.

Even though I was only three I can amazingly ,still recall every second of that morning. Auntie Bettie's heavy Memphis accent got thicker the angrier she got. I usually obeyed this ugly, heavyset elderly woman, her mouth screwed into a perpetual grimace. Her malicious brown eyes glared at me as if I were one of the cockroaches that infested the two-room shack she lived in at the edge of Memphis, Tennessee. But for some reason on that particular morning I defied her by saying, "No!"

3 years old

Auntie Bettie wore baggy cotton housedresses that came

down to below her knees. Around her massive waist she always tied a long, dirty grey apron with two huge pockets. From the minute I met her three weeks earlier after my mom ran away in fear of her life when my dad pressed his old Smith & Wesson pistol to her head, I was frightened to death of this great-auntie who had been forced by the same gun by my dad to take me in. I found out later that my dad had compelled Auntie Bettie to do his bidding.

"Dis kid is livin' wit' ya now," I heard him shout at her. "Tony is yers. Mind wha' I say or I'll com' back an' kill ya!"

Auntie Bettie cowered when he said those words and didn't reply to his threat. But from the way she looked at me as I stood next to him I sensed her hatred at having a little baby abruptly thrust upon her. As I got to know, she was afraid of no one. Although she was only 5'4", her massive bulk towered above me. She had amazing energy and loved to bully and intimidate everyone, including the neighbors. Everyone, that is, except Sam, my dad. She had a really loud voice and marched around like a soldier, stiff and erect. She drank just about every day and was a devout Southern Baptist, attending church on Sundays. Auntie Bettie was ruthless, and it was alleged that she'd taken the lives of a couple of her shady moonshiner associates and buried their bodies deep into the woods. But the authorities were never able to substantiate the allegations.

Auntie taught me a prayer to say every night, but I didn't understand most of the words. I became aware that the prayer was a plea. As soon as we got home from church I'd get a thrashing just for the hell of it, they became part of our daily routine. She'd make me go into the woods to find a suitable tree switch to lash me with. I soon realized, that Auntie Bettie's temper was as vicious and mean as my dad's. There was no love in this woman heart who prayed daily to God. Her whole mind was filled with hate.

She was a widow at the time I was brought to live with her

in 1960. I came to find out she had a hard life. Poverty-stricken, she had lived alone for many years. Her daughter, Alberta, had grown up and moved to St. Louis.

In the small kitchen of her dilapidated shack was her bed, a chair, and an old torn and ripped recliner. Hanging over her bed were a picture of Baby Jesus and a crucifix. A few feet away was an old iron angular wood-burning stove.

I slept in the front room on a wooden cot. Hung on the wall were pictures of Dr. Martin Luther King, Jr. and the two Kennedy brothers, John and Robert. There were boxes and junk everywhere. At night I'd hear the rodents running between the walls. They would occasionally eat their way into the shack. Auntie would set rodent traps to catch them.

The shack was infested with flies and mosquitoes. The walls were covered in wallpaper turned a dirty brownish from the smoke, and thin enough to let in light between the rotting wood exterior. The small front porch, precariously supported by cinder blocks, sagged almost to the bare ground. The floors were covered in cracked, stained linoleum. No electricity or indoor plumbing. Like farmers, we went to bed when it got dark or sat in the light of two kerosene lamps.

The two small, stained flyspecked windows let in hardly any light. The smell of the lamps, the smoke from the stove, the summer heat and humidity combined to turn the place into a hellhole. In the winter it was freezing cold, like an icebox, and I always begged to be allowed to sit near the stove.

There was a pump in the back yard to fill up two tin buckets with water. As soon as I was old enough to carry them, that was one of my daily chores. Another was to feed Auntie's four chickens and collect their eggs. The worst job, though, was the pigpen. We had three pigs inside a makeshift corral that was full of mud, wet straw, and their droppings. Every day I had to go in there to feed them and make sure their trough was filled with water. When it was time, Auntie Bettie would slaughter one of the pigs. She'd hang it up and thrust her knife into its stomach. I'd have to help her with butchering and cleaning the carcass.

We lived on Weaver Road, near a creek. Every time I would cross the little bridge to get to our shack I'd look to see if there were any of those deadly water moccasin snakes swimming around in the creek. I enjoyed throwing rocks in there trying to hit one of them, hoping Auntie Bettie didn't catch me. She would have thrown me into the creek head first!

Behind the shack were thick woods going uphill. Auntie sometimes made me spend the night out there. It was so dark and scary I cried myself to sleep. I'd hear the noises of the wild animals, the foxes, and the wild boars, and hear the snakes slithering nearby. I was so afraid I wouldn't go to relieve myself in the dark, thinking I'd get eaten alive.

Our only neighbor to the right was Miss Bonnie, who, unlike us, lived in a brick house. We were all very poor and considered 'country' because of our Memphis accents and culture.

7 years old

The area was as far away from Elvis Presley's Graceland mansion as Mars was from Earth. Nor were we anywhere near Memphis' famous Beale Street blues and nightlife district, or the Lorraine Motel where Martin Luther King, Jr. was assassinated. The Mississippi River and its water traffic flowed slowly through town, but I knew nothing of its history at the time, not of Mark Twain and his riverboat days in Memphis.

The joy was taken from my little soul the morning that Auntie Bettie held me over the flames. Life, at that moment, forced me to grow up at such a young age. I found the inner strength and faith to put aside my bitterness. As I grew into manhood, I no longer ask myself why. I do know that I became an adult that day at the hands of an evil woman when I was only three years old.

CHAPTER 2

I have no recollection of any talk in my family of being slaves, even though most of us, including me, picked cotton. I know for sure, however, that my ancestors were obviously brought to America, and certainly against their will.

After I had my ancestry researched, I learned that my history reaches back roughly 600 years. That's astonishing. I also learned I am parts African, Native-American, Asian, and French Creole. I might even have Middle-Eastern DNA because my ancient African lineage moved towards the Middle East to follow the great herds of large mammals north through the grassy plains and savannas of the Sahara gateway that leads to Egypt and Libya.

Mae Pearson, in her early 20s

My mom, Daisy Mae Williams, who everyone called Mae, was biracial, half French and half African-American. Born in the tiny town of Ashland, Mississippi, to Ada Patterson and Sandy Harris, my mom was beautiful and had a very light complexion, with a petite figure, and didn't speak with a Southern accent. Like most in the community, she picked cotton before deciding to move to Memphis to find a better life.

The earliest mention I have of my father's family goes

back to 1847 when my great-great-grandfather, Robert Pearson, was born. He had two wives, Ann Gore, with whom he had 12 children, and Angeline, his second wife, with whom he had an additional five children.

Sam Pearson, in his late 40s

My dad, Sam Pearson, was born in 1905 in Rossville, Fayette County, Tennessee, a sleepy town that was originally a farming community. It was established in 1859 and has never had a population of more than 900. Knowing my ambitious, energetic dad, a driving force, I can imagine him leaving there before he was out of his teens. His family, I learned, practiced voodoo. Many of them came from the Caribbean islands, where everyone knew voodoo. The only child of Frances and Rufus Hurdle, he was horribly mistreated as a child. Once he was thrown into the pigpen as a baby because his mother didn't want him. She said he was too black and ugly. Luckily, his Aunt rescued him.

By 1951, Dad had worked his way to Memphis. One fateful day on his work route delivering ice he met Mae. Cutting a grand figure around town with his fancy clothes and cars, he was obnoxious and walked with a swagger. With his usual loud tone he bragged about what he had to anyone who would listen. He knew how to turn on the charm and he impressed Mae.

Elegant, intelligent and vibrant, she had already been married at the age of 16 and had a son, Eddie, who lived with his father after she and her husband divorced. When she met my dad, Mom was barely out of her teens. Sam was a single father of a daughter, Ruby Nell, who was living at her own mother's house.

By 1952 Sam and Mae were married. During the early

years they appeared to be the typical all-American family as the children came along. The oldest daughter, Shirley, was born in 1954, Sam, Jr. in 1955, and Carolyn in 1956. But as Dad's alcohol abuse worsened he showed a far darker side to his personality, one he had kept hidden. The Pearson's home life took a drastic turn and he began his brutal, nightly rampage, lashing out against Mom. He was no kinder to his own mother, either, as he assaulted her on many occasions. Mom told me later how she had witnessed him beating her. Dad's overpowering presence instilled fear into everyone. They were intimidated by him. He had a deep, baritone voice and used it at the top of its range when he was angry.

When I was born, in 1957, Dad's uncontrollable anger continued. Several times over the years he had threatened to kill my mom. She would later confide to me that she wanted to run away so badly, but she couldn't face leaving us children, especially after I was born. When Dad came home from work as usual he went straight into the kitchen and he'd start yelling about his dinner not being ready, and complaining about me. I cried a lot as a baby, most likely as a result of the tension in the house.

"I though' I toldya my dinne' betta be ready when I git home." He shouted from the kitchen if it wasn't prepared. He'd throw his lunch pail on the kitchen counter, open the icebox, and take out a bottle of beer. Then he'd call at the top of his voice.

"Shirley, git yer lil' butt in here."

She rushed and stood in the kitchen doorway, fidgety as she shook one leg. "Yes, daddy," the six-year-old would squeak.

I'd start crying loudly again and screaming, probably from fright.

"How many time," yelled my dad, "do I gotta tellya ta keep dat damn boy quiet. I just 'bout had nuff of all y'all. If ya cain't keep him quiet den I gonna shut him up foe good. Now, git yer ass back in der' an' shut dat boy up."

"Yes sir, daddy." My sister said fearfully.

"Mae, wher' da hell are ya?" Screamed my dad.

A few moments later, Mom entered the kitchen with her soft voice, said, "Dinner will be ready in a few minutes, Sam."

Without warning, Dad snapped. He ripped off his sunglasses, threw them on the kitchen table, and punched Mom in the face. He knocked her to the floor, climbed on top of her, and kept up the punching as hard as he could with his fist. Then, with both hands he began to choke her and slam her head repeatedly on the floor, fracturing her cheekbone and blackening both of her eyes during the attack.

"I toldya' I'm gonna kill ya!" he shouted. "Taday, ya bitch, I gonna fuckin' kill ya, ya whore! I killed a fuckin' nigga befoe. I knifed da son' bitch ta death. Killin' ya mean nothin' ta me. I promise ya, ya gonna be dead. Ya ain't nuthin' but a fuckin' slut."

"Sam, please stop! Please, what did I do? Get off me. Help! Help! Someone please help me!" She cried out.

My dad finally stopped striking her and said, "Now git yer ass up."

Mom stood up, disheveled, wiping the blood from her battered mouth, eyes, and nose. As he always did, he blamed her afterwards, yelling, "Ya bitch, see whatya made me do."

Mom, sobbing, said, "Why do you hate me so much? What have I ever done to you? Oh, my God, please help me!"

"Ya disgus' me. Git over der' an' fix me my damn plate." He said with a hateful tone.

Mom was trembling uncontrollably as she made his plate and placed it in front of him on the kitchen table. "Here's your dinner, Sam," she painfully mumbled.

I guess I was still crying in my crib because, according to Mom, the next thing my dad said to her was, "Ya betta git yer high yella ass in der' an' shut da baby up. He screamin' all da fuckin' time. I had 'bout enuff wit dis damn noise. I toldya I didn't won't no mo' damn chil'en."

Then, with his rage being spent, while sitting calmly at the kitchen table, he put his sunglasses back on and ate his dinner as if nothing had happened.

My Dad made a good living as an ice and coal deliveryman with his own truck. There were no refrigerators back then, only iceboxes, and he worked a six- day week fulfilling all the orders. He made enough money to buy a real nice five-bedroom house in a trendy part of town. Dad wore expensive clothes and drove new cars. He bought us nice clothes and lots of toys. My dad's signature was a pair of dark sunglasses he always wore, day and night, and his favorite expression was "Whaddya do?" (meaning "How are you doing?"). Like most in the African-American community, he spoke in a real deep Southern dialect that goes back to the early 1900s, especially in Memphis, and remains so to this day. My mom disclosed to me later how my dad came home one day intoxicated and irate because he'd heard that she was seeing another man. She said how he'd attacked her. She continued by saying that he'd knocked her to the floor under a barrage of blows and how he repeatedly kicked her in the stomach even though he knew she was pregnant. He reminded her again how he'd already taken another man's life and was for sure going to kill her, too. Then he suddenly blurted out how he disappeared, hiding out with relatives in Chicago to escape law enforcement before returning back to Memphis to serve his time. Mom said that she didn't want to believe him, that she thought it was just the alcohol talking at the time, and that he was boasting about killing someone. Just the thought of hearing that my dad had committed such a heinous crime shook my mom up terribly, she said, because she couldn't imagine it.

Dad never mistreated my sisters Shirley, Carolyn, or my half-sister Janice when she visited. He adored his daughters and treated them as if they were angels. Nor did he hit me, as I was still a baby. But Dad was so unpredictable in his mood swings.

One night it all came to a head after he'd pressed a hand-gun at my mom's throat, vowing to do what he should've done years ago. Afraid for her life, my Mom knew it was time to leave. Just after midnight, after my dad had fallen asleep, my mom was crying as she, Shirley, Carolyn, and Sam, Jr., with Mom carrying me, tip-toed quietly out of the front door with a large suitcase and some money she had taken out of Dad's wallet and took a taxi to her cousin's home. Because of the late hour, with her carrying a large suitcase and us kids shivering in the cold night air, the taxi driver asked if she was running away.

"Yes," she told him. "I am."

"You seem to be happy," the taxicab driver said.

"I sure am," she replied.

❖ ❖ ❖

Pretty soon Dad found out where she was living. He came to see her and promised to change.

"No, I'm not coming back," Mom told him.

"Every thang gonna be betta. I'll change," he said. "I promise."

"No, we're done! Give me 25 cents to buy some milk for the baby." Mom had just lost her baby-sitting job. She had no money to buy food and we weren't eating.

"I'm not givin' ya nutin.'" He told her.

Dad left angry, but a neighbor, an older man, had overheard the conversation and gave her the money. Each time he saw her thereafter he'd give her a dime or a quarter. Even that small amount of money went a long way back in those days. Eventually, Dad persuaded Mom to come back, promising that he'd changed.

She believed him and Mom and the kids all returned home. But within a few months Dad was worse than ever. After enduring more of his agonizing pummeling, she knew her life was in great danger and she ran away again after more death threats. This time she had to leave all of us children behind because it was her only chance to escape. She promised my sister Shirley that after she had gotten settled she'd return for us.

If Dad was livid before, it was nothing compared to his wrath when he found out Mom had left. Because he had to stay home to take care of us kids he realized he couldn't go to work and that turned his anger against us. I guess that's when he decided he needed to split us up to live with his various relatives.

With my luck I was forced upon my great-Auntie Bettie. Did my dad know she was elderly, poor, and totally unfit to raise a little baby? It was a heartless environment to leave me in as surely he knew she had an awful temper. And that she drank as much as he did. I never have figured out why he was always so cruel. Even at a tender age of three I'd never seen my dad smile or for that matter, heard him laugh.

Mom went back to her relatives, who lived in an upscale neighborhood. Dad tracked her down there. When she saw him asking around about her, Mom called the cops. Two Caucasian policemen arrived and told him that if they ever caught him again in the neighborhood, they'd take care of him. They saw that he was much older than my mom and they just probably thought he was up to no good, especially after they saw she was a cute little half-Caucasian young woman. That put an end to his search. My dad never went back. I guess he realized the cops were serious, and that he'd better let it go.

As time passed, Dad became a full–blown alcoholic,

friendless, poverty-stricken, dying alone of colon cancer. At his funeral his own Aunt Ava cursed him, calling him an evil son of a bitch, and hoping he'd burn in hell. My sister, Shirley, revealed to me the horrific suffering he went through as she'd visited him at the hospital, how she could hear him down the hall, screaming from pain because of this deadly disease that had taken over his body. Not even the extreme amounts of morphine he was given had any effect. He'd continuously asked for Mae, begging to see her and some of the time he had mistaken my sister as being Mom. When my sister told mom what had happened, Mom thought about it and decided not to visit him.

CHAPTER 3

O ur family household in Memphis had always been in great turmoil, but my life got far worse when I went to live with my great-Auntie Bettie. She looked like an old lady but was only in her late fifties. Tough as nails and as powerful as a bull, she worked plowing the fields with the horses, picking cotton and occasionally acting as a lookout for moonshiners. And she was known for dishonest dealings with everyone. Born in 1904, in Rossville, Fayette County, Tennessee, her parents had been sharecroppers, like many African-American families at the time.

The day my dad brought me to her old two-room place, he was dressed very stylishly in black slacks, a white shirt, and a black jacket. He was wearing black alligator shoes, and, of course, his dark sunglasses. When we went into Auntie Bettie's shack, it was so gloomy and hot he had to take the sunglasses off. He used his handkerchief to wipe his face.

"Hey, Bettie. Whaddya do?" He asked her with his familiar greeting.

"I'ma gittin' along," she answered, "What goin' on witya? Ya ain't lookin' ta good."

At those words, Dad's face turned into an evil mask. "Yeah! I gotta problem. Shit, dat bitch Mae left me. She ran off last nigh' wit another' main. What am I gonna do wit all dem damn chil'en? I cain't go ta work. I could end up losin' da house, da cars. Every damn thang. Wait til I git my hands on dat whore. I need ya ta take da youngest boy. Da othe' three I gonna keep foe now cuz deys gonna be startin' skool soon. Ya know Tony, righ'? He da baby boy."

The two walked into the kitchen and I followed behind, hoping I could go back home with my Dad. Auntie Bettie looked at me and said, "No, Sam, I cain't. I really don't won't him. I'm too ol' an' tire' ta tryin' ta be raisin' a lil' baby. C'mon, Sam, ya cain't put dat burden on me."

With no warning he grabbed her by the throat and shoved her into a corner, pulling his gun from his pocket, and pointing it in her face. He repeated that if he couldn't work he would lose everything, saying that if he could kick the shit out of his own Mama, he would do worse to her.

"Ya betta git dat through yer head, ol' lady," he shouted. "Ya might fuck wit othe' folks but ya don' mess wit me. I ain't fuckin' aroun'. I'm da boss round here."

I could only surmise that she was petrified, realizing she was no match for his insanity. When she hastily agreed to take me, he released her. Still agitated, he paced back and forth across the worn linoleum. Dad was beyond furious. I was shaking so badly, I peed myself thinking he just might kill this fat, ugly old woman right in front of me.

"One mo' fuckin' thang," he said, taking her by her throat again while fist-pumping his chest. "I'm warnin' ya, don' let dat no-good bitch take dat baby from dis house or ya gonna pay wit yer fuckin' life. Ya got dat?"

"Yes, sir, Sam!" Said Auntie fearfully.

Without a backward glance at me, not even a goodbye, my Dad hurried out of the shack and drove away in his truck. I just stood in the middle of the room, scarcely daring to look at Auntie Bettie after I'd heard her say she didn't want me there. I felt tears running down my face, but I said nothing. After leaving our big beautiful house to live in this dirty rotten shack, I guess I was in shock at the turn of events.

A week or so after my dad left me with my great-aunt, I heard a knock on the door and a voice calling out. "Miss Bettie, are you in there? I'm Mae Pearson. Please, I was wondering if I could see my baby?"

My mother's voice! Joy swept through me and I rushed to the door as fast as my little naked feet would carry me. My nightmare was over. Mom had come to take me home! I was so excited I fell against Auntie. I tried to squeeze between her legs but they were as thick and as sturdy as if made of oak.

"Mama! Mama!" I called out.

Auntie Bettie brutally pushed me away and yelled out to Mom, "What da hell ya doin' down here?"

She yanked open the door and stood in the doorway facing Mom in a menacing stance with her hands on her hips. "Git the hell outta here, ya whore! Sam told me how ya ran off wit' anothe' main. What kinda lowlife mothe' would leave her own chil'en like dat?"

"No, it's not true, Miss Bettie. You know how vindictive Sam is. I never wanted to leave my children. This is killing me! Sam and I had some serious issues that forced me to leave him. How is my baby?" My mom cried out.

"Tony doin' jes fine." Auntie responded.

"Please let me see him. I have some toys and clothes for him."

I glanced down at my shirt and pants, three sizes too big because I was a tiny little kid and the clothes had belonged to my older brother. But I didn't care about clothes or toys, I just wanted to go home with my mom. When I began tugging again at Auntie long dress, she kicked me viciously aside with just one push of her leg and continued to shout.

"No, ya cain't see him. I don't won't yer clothes. Ya not

welcom' down here." I could see Auntie Bettie was getting very perturbed. "I don' wanna hea' no mo of yer cotton-pickin' lies. Now git yer ass off my porch," she said as she slammed the door.

I could hear Mom's sobs as she pounded on the decaying wood panels. It was a long time before she finally gave up. "It's all right, Tony," she called out. "I'll be back."

Auntie Bettie picked me up in her mighty arms as if I were a feather and threw me out the back door.

CHAPTER 4

Mom's next trip, she told me later, was to a Memphis lawyer's office to help her reclaim us children. She wanted full custody because of my dad's violence.

John Lewis was a 6'0", Caucasian, in his 60s, and with a full head of gray hair. With a reputation for honesty and respect, he'd been practicing law for 30 years and was considered one of the best attorneys in Memphis. He came well recommended and Mom had high hopes of getting us back. She began telling him her story.

"In the beginning my husband Sam was very attentive and caring. We were happy together. I had no idea why his personality began to change. Then it seemed as if I was living with a man I didn't know." Mom paused and took out a handkerchief from her purse to wipe away the tears, then continued, "He became very abusive and controlling."

"How long did this go on?" Asked Lewis.

"Several years. It got worse and worse."

"Was it both mental and physical?"

"Yes, sir. He'd call me every degrading name you can imagine. It was extremely hurtful. Finally, I just couldn't take it anymore. I was scared to death of him. He threatened my life numerous times, especially when he was drinking, which was most of the time. I remember this one occasion that I'll never forget, how he severely assaulted me, putting me into the hospital. But that wasn't the worst he's done. He told to me he'd killed a man years earlier. I thought it was just the alcohol talking."

"How did you determine that it was the truth?" Said the lawyer.

"Because after he'd told me I checked it out. It was true, he had killed a man over practically nothing, my husband, he's an ex-con. After he'd revealed this, I was horrified, so I knew I had no choice but to escape during the night. Now, sir, I need to get my children back!"

"Tell me their names," said Lewis.

As she recited the information, he wrote it down, then said, "I don't understand, Miss Pearson. Why can't you just go over there to his home and retrieve them?"

Mom explained that it was complicated, that her husband had taken me, her baby, to his aunt Bettie's house in the woods way out in the country.

"She won't even allow me to see him. I'm not sure where the others are. I'm at my wit's end. It's a complete mess. Can you please help me?"

As she wept, Lewis looked at her. His empathy was obvious, and he tried to assure her he'd do his best to help. "I will surely take your case, ma'am," he said. "In my opinion, you stand a very good chance of getting your children back, considering your tempestuous marriage history."

The two shook hands and I could only guess my Mom left his office with a much lighter heart filled with hope than when she'd arrived. Lewis told her he would start filing for custody immediately. She hadn't been sure whether to consult an attorney for her situation or not but soon realized it was the only safe, sure and legal way to get back the children. Sadly, she was wrong on all counts.

As soon as Dad received the custody petition from Mom's attorney, John Lewis, he went to consult with his own lawyer, David Warner. A short Caucasian man in his 50s, he was overweight, balding, and a chain smoker with a penchant for three-piece suits. Having been in practice for 35 years, he was a familiar face in the local courts, carefully crafting business relationships with judges that often proved beneficial to his clients.

Warner was a good friend of my dad's, it was made known to me later, and their conversation went something like this:

"Hey, David," said my Dad. "Whaddya do?"

David replied back. "I'm doing great, and you?"

"Thangs ain't so good. Mae done gone run off wit another' main. Left me wit all dem damn chil'en. Now she tryin' ta get'em back. She went out an' hired a lawyer. Well, I gotta be in court dis month. The problem is, I took da youngest boy ta da country, ta my Auntie Bettie's house, an' dat wher' he gonna stay. I need ya ta take care of dis. We cain't let Mae make dat court date."

Warner was a little hesitant. He sat in thought for a moment, then said, "I've known you for a long time, Sam. You're a good friend. I've always been in your corner. But, I don't know about this one. We're dealing with children here." He went quiet for a few seconds and then said. "Perhaps, I can persuade my judge friend to postpone the date," He paused to stub out his cigarette and lit another one he took from a pack on his desk. "We could keep stalling the case, impede its progress, you know what I'm saying? Eventually, she's sure to give up. I'm certain we can make this little problem disappear. But it's gonna cost you, Sam."

"How much we talkin' bout here?"

"About $1,500, and, by the way," the lawyer added with a

wink, "this conversation never took place."

"Ya ain't gotta worry bout dat." My Dad's deep voice got louder. "It won' leave dis room. I don't care what it take. I jes wanna make sho' dat no-good, unfit wife of mine never git dem damn chil'en back."

He got up to leave and the two shook hands. As Dad went out the door Warner called after him, "In the meantime, take care of yourself. You look a mess!"

CHAPTER 5

A few days after her visit to John Lewis' office, Mom made a second attempt to see me and take me home with her. I heard the exact kind of timid, knock on the shack door as she'd made the first time, and I felt the same rush of jubilation as before. But the visit was as fruitless as the first. Auntie Bettie aggressively opened the door, she was incensed at the sight of my mom. Her large body filled the entrance. I could hear Mom outside pleading to see me as she stood in the pouring rain.

"Miss Bettie, please hear me out. I know you're not pleased with this unfortunate situation that you've been put in. I'm very sorry. This is extremely painful for me. I just want my baby. Is there any chance you could give him to me?"

Auntie Bettie, hateful of my mom and fearful of my dad if she went against his demands, answered with a loud, forceful tone.

"No! Dat boy ain't goin' nowhere. I aint' got nuthin' mo' ta say ta ya. Ya ain't allowed down here. I toldya da las' time not ta com' back." Her voice got louder as she shouted, "Now, ya listen ta me. If ya evah sho' yer half-breed ass down here 'gain, I gonna take my shotgun an' blow yer damn head off! Don't thank I won't."

She leaned down behind the door and grabbed her shotgun pointing the barrel at Mom. Mom who then, scared to death of Auntie's threat, stepped back a few paces.

"Now git yer yella ass off my porch!"

Desperately Mom implored, wiping the rainwater from her face while gesturing at Auntie. "Miss Bettie, this isn't right. Please, have a heart. I'm begging you! This is my baby boy we're talking about!"

"Ya shoulda though' 'bout dat befoe' ya start screwin' round wit all dem otha' men."

As Auntie said the last words she loudly shut the door. I could hear Mom crying on the other side.

Listening to her was one of the worst moments of my life, though I was still a toddler at the time. I will never forget the agony, standing there mute with angry tears rolling down my face, staring at my Auntie, wishing her dead. Feeling the pain in my little heart, much too young to fully express these emotions. To this day, I can still see the scene in my mind as vivid as a movie: fat old Auntie Bettie screaming as she stood at the doorway, holding the shotgun, and Mom's sweet voice beseeching her to give me up.

It got quiet and Auntie went back into the kitchen to tend to the pot of soup she was cooking. Still standing there, I tried in vain to hear my Mom's voice and realized, after some time, she had left. I remained on the floor right inside the front door for hours hoping that she would come back and take me home with her. I shut down as if the world had gone away and all this madness wasn't actually happening. I don't think I had any feeling left in my little soul right then, not even as I felt lost and abandoned. I would never escape from this wicked woman; I'd been consigned to hell.

If I was terrified the time when Auntie Bettie held me over the flames, I remembered the deep fear that came over me wondering how much she'd release her fury on me this time. I'm sure she'd have loved to have given me up to Mom and gotten rid of me. She hated having to raise a little baby and she made that clear everyday with her dreadful moods. It was only as I grew older that I understood the dynamics of the situation. But I never forgave the woman for her cruelty, especially toward my mom.

My life continued on with Auntie Bettie's yelling, the semi-starvation and my poverty-stricken existence. I was never fed more than one meal a day and that was usually pig chitterlings and any produce that grew in the garden. Often corn bread and molasses was my entire meal. No milk, nor protein. Auntie chewed tobacco and spat out the brown juice all over the place, some of it deliberately landing on my food.

The only contact we had with people was when we attended church each Sunday, but even then we never spoke to anyone. I guess Auntie Bettie's grumpy face and demeanor kept everyone away. Sometimes I was asked if I'd like to have a soda and a cookie after the service, but Auntie always refused to allow me to accept anything.

CHAPTER 6

Mom told me later that she waited several weeks for her attorney to call her, but no message arrived. Finally, she went to his office.

"Hi, Mr. Lewis, how are you?" Said Mom.

"I'm doing good. Miss Pearson, nice to see you, please, have a seat."

"Thank you. I was wondering if you have any information about my case."

Lewis picked up a pen and twirled it around his fingers. Without looking at her, he said, "I'm very sorry but unfortunately there are some unforeseen issues in scheduling your case. It was removed from the calendar on a number of occasions for some unknown reasons."

"But you were so positive when I first came here," Mom said. "You said it would go forward without any delay." Mom began to cry.

"Please don't cry, ma'am, don't worry," said Lewis. "I will remain steadfast and inform you as soon as I have something more concrete as to an exact date."

"You don't sound hopeful. Please, I must get my children back, sir!"

Lewis stood up to indicate the meeting was over. He came

from behind his desk and walked her toward the door. "Miss Pearson, I understand your deep concern, but I promise you, I am doing all I can to take care of this matter. Now, please try to remain calm. I will contact you soon."

Mom left John Lewis' office and never heard from him again. She said she was convinced Dad had gotten to her attorney somehow and scared him off. Either, he paid him a visit himself to threaten him or sent one of his criminal friends to do so.

CHAPTER 7

At six years old it was time for me to start school. We knew I was six because Auntie Bettie received a letter from the Weaver Road elementary school informing her that she needed to enroll me. My Auntie had found some secondhand clothes and shoes for me at the church that parishioners donated and I wore them proudly. I'd never been around other kids since I'd come to live with my Auntie three years earlier. I felt terrified with the thought of starting school because I had no idea how to interact with other children. The only thing I'd learned from Auntie was how to keep my emotions and thoughts to myself, keep my mouth shut, and how to promptly say yes ma'am and no ma'am.

School opened up a whole new world for me. That first day was typical Auntie. She walked me the two miles to school, found the first-grade classroom, handed me over to the teacher and told me as she stormed out and left, "Ya can find yer own way home."

The teacher said nothing, but I could see her disapproval, even shock, at my Auntie's behavior. I wondered if this was how my Auntie had treated her own daughter when she started school.

The first few days of school were nerve-wracking. I was totally lacking in social development. In the school playground I was shy and lost, not knowing what to say or do. I watched the other kids as if they were from another planet. They laughed and joked, played noisy games and shouted with each other, seeming to have so much fun while I stood silently by, isolated and alone. Some of them were sharing comics with each other and I wished I could join them. It took many weeks before I felt comfortable enough to talk to my classmates.

Constant malnourishment became an even bigger problem when school started. Knowing Auntie Bettie I believe she enjoyed the fact that I was suffering from hunger as another means of control. I'd hoped and prayed that on this particular morning she would make me breakfast. I was so lightheaded I could barely stand up and I knew the long walk to school would be impossible. As I mumbled, I tried to get Auntie's sympathy.

"Auntie, I won' somethin' ta eat befoe I go. I'm really hongry."

"No," she said. She was sitting sewing in her beige recliner. It was the only decent piece of furniture in the shack, but there were rips and cracks in the vinyl. "Don'tya git a free lunch at skool?"

"Yes, ma'am, but da walk is real far. By da time I git der I feel like I gonna pass out. My stomach hurt. I cain't wait til' lunch ta eat. I cain't focus on my skool work."

Auntie completely went to town after I said that, saying she'd walked ten miles to school, which I didn't believe for a moment, and that I was just a little lazy ass ungrateful bastard.

"Stop yer whinin'," she yelled, "or I gonna keep yer ass home foe da rest of da week. I got people watchin' ya. If dae tell me ya been talkin' ta somebod', I gonna beat ya ta death, now git da hell outta my face."

Obviously, she was still frightened that my dad might hear some negative reports and make good on his threat to kill her. Now that I understand the circumstances, I can't comprehend the sense of it. If he followed through with it, what would he do with me? Where would I go? With his crazy mindset and temper his threats were his way of exerting power and control over Auntie.

My teachers regularly told me I was smart but I didn't do well with my classes, deprived of nutrition I founded it difficult to focus on what the teachers were saying. My reading and writing skills fell way behind the other kids and at one point I had to repeat a class. No mystery about that after what I'd been going through. As I grew older I was diagnosed with dyslexia. There was no such thing as a book in Auntie Bettie's shack. We would once in while watch TV at Miss Bonnie's house next door for update of the news.

Subjected to daily psychological abuse at home made it impossible to find any success at school. But I persisted. I began making new friends and learning more about the world outside of the shack. At the age of nine, loathing my predicament, I started to run away from home and sought refuge with my classmates' families. But Auntie always found me.

It would take two or three days, but she would find out where I was and she would come and take me back. Striding menacingly towards my classmate's house, her chest heaving with rage, yelling her head off. No one was brave enough to stand up to her.

She never said a word as I followed her home each time, trying to keep up with her heavy tread as she stomped down the country dirt roads. My heart would pound in my chest because I knew when we got home she would release a vicious assault on me, beating me worse than ever.

The third and last time I ran away, the parents made my Auntie promise she wouldn't hit me if they allowed me to go home with her. By the mercy of God, she agreed. She kept that promise. She didn't hit me. Instead she starved me for two days as punishment. And I was forced from sunrise to sunset with the backbreaking task of cutting down trees and chopping them into blocks for the cook stove.

At this point, I knew I had reached bottom. My spirit was broken. I no longer had faith or hope that my situation would ever change. I envisioned living my life of hell forever. Trapped and alone, I accepted the fact that no one was coming to save me, not even my mom. It had been five years since she tried to take me back. For all I knew, my dad had already killed her.

Not too long after starting school Auntie made me beg strangers for money. As I walked home from school, I would ask people for a quarter, mortified but knowing I had no choice. Some days I was unable to get any money and on those days the walk down Weaver Road was a long, slow, sad affair preparing myself for a severe lashing that I'd receive when I arrived home.

Luckily, one day, I met an African-American gentleman with a limp walking ahead of me. He looked kindly and I approached him. "Excuse me, sir," I said. "Can ya please gimme twenty-five cent?"

"Why do ya need twenty-five cent? Don't ya folks giv' ya money?" He asked, wiping the sweat from his face with a rag. "What's yer name? Mine's Calvin."

I muttered in reply, "My name's Tony, an' we ain't got no money. If I don' com' home wit sum money, I gonna git a beatin.'"

"Who beats ya?"

I stared at the ground, embarrassed. "My Auntie."

"How often do dis go on?" Calvin asked.

"Everyday. I run away but she always fin' me."

"Where's yer Mama and Daddy?"

"I don' know. I been livin' wit my Auntie since I was a baby." Calvin stared at me. I could see the compassion in his eyes.

"I feel sorr' foe ya, boy. I wis' der' was somein' I could do. It pains me. I wis' I could help ya but it's an unspoken rule down here ta keep yer nose outta otha' folks' bidness if ya don' wont trouble. The lease I can do, son, is giv' ya fifty cent."

He reached into his pocket and drew out two quarters. I was thrilled. I thanked him over and over before we said good-bye to each other. When I gave the money to Auntie Bettie she didn't say a word, and threw it in an old coffee can she kept her money in.

CHAPTER 8

When I was ten years old my Auntie Bettie's daughter, Alberta, came for her annual visit in the late Fall. In her mid-30s, she was the spitting image of her mother with none of her anger. Like her mother, Alberta did enjoy drinking, mostly moonshine, cheap whisky, or Colt 45.

Alberta was quiet, wore glasses, and seemed genuinely kind-hearted. *Maybe, with her staying with us*, I thought, *I wouldn't get a whipping*. The second day of her visit, Auntie fed me practically nothing, *Perhaps she forgot*, I thought.

That evening I came into the front room where Alberta and Auntie were drinking and engaging in conversation. Timidly, I asked "Auntie Bettie, I'm hongry. I need ta eat somethin'. Can I please git dinna?"

Auntie forcefully put down her beer bottle and jumped up, instantly raging. "Git me my damn belt! I told ya not ta be axin' me foe food."

I went into the kitchen and took down her belt that was hanging on a hook. I handed it to her, dreading what was coming.

"Drop yer pants. Bend over an' grab yer damn ankles."

She began violently thrashing my backside with the belt. I knew better than to cry out. That would only make her beat me harder. Tears of pain ran down my face. Quickly, Alberta leapt from her chair and grabbed the belt. She tried to take it away from Auntie but her mother's grip was too tight.

"Mama," she said, "please stop! It's enough. You've gone too far." Auntie Bettie stopped for a moment, turned to her daughter, and shook the belt in her face.

"Ya betta da hell step down," Auntie said angrily. "Don't ya tell me what do. I will turn dis belt on yer ass. Ya brang yer butt down here once a year. I gotta deal wit dis lil' bastard ever' day. Don't ya tell me how ta raise dis boy."

Auntie turned back to hitting me until it seemed she was completely exhausted and dropped into her recliner. I pulled up my pants, but she wasn't done with me yet.

"Ya ain't gettin' nothin' ta eat tonite'," she yelled. "I tell ya when ya gonna eat. Now git yer ass outdos. Ya gonna spend da nite out yonder. I don't wanna see yer ugly face."

"Yes, ma'am," I said, sobbing. "Please don't make me stay out der. It's freezin' cold."

As she shook her finger at me, said, "Boy! If ya open yer mouth one mo' time, I swear ta God I gonna strang yer lil' black ass up in da woods so nobody can findya. Now git da hell outta here."

I was wearing a pair of ragged jeans, a filthy T-shirt, and shoes with holes in the bottom. I was only allowed to wear socks with my shoes for school and church. It was pitch dark when I went outside, but then the clouds moved in and the brisk wind howled. The full moon shone brightly through the trees. I walked a fair distance from the shack until I reached the edge of the woods. I knelt down and put my hands together to pray. I said the words that Auntie Bettie had taught me, despite the fact that I didn't understand all of them.

"Dear God, if ya can hea' my plea, Lord, please hav' mercy on my soul. Yea, though I walk through da valley of da shadow of death, I will fear no evil: Foe Thou art wit me. Thy rod an' thy staff, dae comfort me. Thou anoint my head wit' oil; My cup runneth over. Surely, goodness an' mercy, shall folla me all da days of my life. An' I will dwell in da house of da Lord foe ever. Dear God, please save me. Why must I live through dis misery? If dis is yer will, my God, den let it be done. Amen."

I crept back to the shack and sat outside until I could hear Auntie's loud snores. When I figured it was safe, I went inside and got into my cot. It would be another forty years before the answer to my prayer would reveal itself.

CHAPTER 9

I t was about 4 a.m. when Auntie made me get up and get dressed, saying, "Hurry yer ass up we goin' ta da cotton field." I was still half asleep but rushed to get dressed as I was instructed. When we left home the temperature was already around 90 degrees and the humidity was just as high. It would rise to over 100 degrees as the day wore on.

For picking cotton, Auntie Bettie wore her apron like she always did over a long, loose dress. But this time the oversized pockets were filled with small towels to wipe the sweat off her face when the blistering sun reached its highest point. On her feet were black work boots. I had black boots on, too, and ragged denim overalls. Both of us wore straw hats.

Auntie and I walked a mile on the back dirt roads to the street where a dilapidated bus picked up the field workers. It took an hour or more to reach our destination across the neighboring state line and into Mississippi. It was stuffy inside the bus, with every seat filled and no air conditioning. Most of the riders fell asleep during the journey.

After we got off the bus we stood in line to get a huge cotton sack with a strap to hang over our shoulders and chests. The sacks were made of a rough thick material. It could hold 100lbs. of cotton and I was told to fill it up every day. I was still short for my age and the sack trailed way down past my feet. You could have fit two of me into it.

"Git yer sack on righ' now!" said Auntie Bettie. "I gonna start out a lil' head of ya, an' ya'd betta keep up. I mean it. Dere's mo den fifty people out here an' I don't wanna lose ya in da crowd. An' don't ya be axin' foe food, either. We aint' eatin' nothin' til' noon."

"We ain't ate nutin' dis mornin'. I'm hongry." I said whining. It was my usual, daily grievance and I got the same answer every time.

"Shut yer damn mouth befoe I put my foot in yer butt." She added, shaking me violently, "An' if ya don't pick a hunded pound of cotton by six tonite, I gonna beat yer lil' ass til' ya cain't sit down when we git home."

She led me to a row of cotton in one of the fields that seemed to stretch as far as the horizon. "Pick dis row righ' here," she barked. "Make sho' ya fill up da sack, if ya know what good foe ya."

The cotton plants towered over my head and I picked bolls as high as I could reach. It was back-breaking work and painful. Within ten minutes my fingers and hands were bleeding from the sharp burrs and the thorns on the plants, but I knew better than to ask for pity. After twelve hour days under the burning sun, oftentimes I was unable to fill the sack as I was ordered.

At lunchtime we walked over to the truck area, dragging our cotton sacks with us, to get some water and open the brown paper bags with sandwiches we'd brought from home. Our brief break didn't stop Auntie from yelling at me. "Hurry up. Pull dat sack over here behind da truck."

"It too heavy, Auntie," I said, struggling to do as she demanded. The sack was getting pretty full because, unlike a few of the pickers, I never stopped to talk to anyone or slacken my pace. Auntie grabbed me as hard as she could by my ear and twisted it, pushing my head down towards the ground. There were several workers standing around and watching, but that didn't deter her. With her size and angry, intimidating body language, no one had the nerve to challenge her. "Dat sack ain't heavy. Look like ya ain't got nothin' in der. Ya know what gonna happen when we git back home."

"Yes, ma'am," I stammered. "I'm sorry. I'm tryin' real hard. It too hot out here. I cain't hardly breathe."

Auntie Bettie finally allowed me to get up and let go of my ear. "I was gonna let ya go ta skool tomorra but now look at ya, ya done gone an' made me mad. Ya gonna be out here foe da rest of da week."

When our sacks were full we'd take them to the truck to be weighed and emptied. I dragged my sack along the rows where I'd see some pickers crawling along on their knees as they picked because their back pain was so severe after years of bending over. It was a sad sight but one that was repeated all over the cotton fields in the deep South.

One afternoon, after several weeks of picking, there was a knock on the door. No one hardly ever came by and I'd given up praying for someone to come and rescue me. Auntie Bettie snatched the door open. I heard a man's voice say, "Are you the guardian for Tony Pearson?"

Auntie opened the door wider, and I managed to stand at her side as she stood in a confrontational posture, with her chest stuck out. "Yes. How can I help ya?"

The man was a middle-aged African-American with a thin build and wearing glasses. I knew who he was as I'd seen him at school. In response to my Auntie's ferocious glare he wrote something on the clipboard he was carrying.

"I am Mr. Jackson, the school principal," he said, somewhat uneasily. "I'm here to inquire about Tony. He hasn't been to school for over two and a half months."

"I know dat!" Auntie almost spat the words. "He got ta work wit me in da cotton fields. Somebod' gotta help me survive round here. So do me a favor, sir. Don't com' down here botherin' me wit all dis nonsense. Ya need ta git yer skinny ass outta my yard."

"Miss Pearson, it's against the law," said Mr. Jackson, "to prevent this child from attending school. I'm going to have to report you to the authorities and I will make certain you lose custody of the child."

Auntie was livid at the man's threat. "Ya go head. I got my shotgun righ' here." She grabbed the shotgun from behind the door and held it at her side. "I ain't afraid of nobod', so write dat down on yer clipboard, mister. If ya gonna send sombod' down here ta fuck wit me, I got somethin' foe'em. Ya gotta a lot of nerve foe a lil' main. Ya betta git yer cheap suit-wearin' ass offa my porch." She screamed.

Auntie then stepped back into the shack and slammed the door in his face. I knew there'd be no consequences to Auntie's behavior by the authorities. The police were all Caucasians and couldn't care less about some little African-American child. Auntie Bettie knew that. The man left and the next day I went back to school. Having missed two and a half months of classes I tried my best to catch up but without much success.

CHAPTER 10

One day when I was out in the back yard chopping wood, Auntie Bettie came to the back door of the shack and summoned me, telling me to get dressed in my Sunday best. This consisted of black slacks, a white shirt, a white bow tie, and shiny black patent dress shoes. This is what I wore to the Baptist church every Sunday, but this was Wednesday and I wondered about the reason for wearing my good clothes. When I asked her she told me that we were going over to Miss Bonnie's to watch a speech on television by Dr. Martin Luther King, Jr.

Miss Bonnie was in her mid-30s, soft-spoken, nice and very smart. She and her husband had lived next door for years but they were recently divorced and now she lived alone. She was always sociable and often invited us over, but Auntie would normally refused the offer. Not this time. She decided our visit was a dress-up day because of Dr. King.

"Boy! Git yer ass in here an' put yer Sunday clothes on," she said.

"Yes, ma'am," I replied.

"We goin' over ta Miss Bonnie's ta watch Dr. King giv' a speech here in Memphis. Boy, befoe we git over der I warnin' ya, I gonna beat yer ass righ' in front of her. Ya betta not sit on a chair. Ya sit yer ass on da floor in a corner, an' only speak when ya spoken ta. Don' go axin' foe somethin' ta eat. If ya gotta go ta da pot, ya betta hold it."

Auntie always knew how to kill any happiness or excitement I might have about going over to Miss Bonnie's house. Visiting next door was a treat for me because we never went anywhere except to the market, school, and church. Miss Bonnie was the only neighbor Auntie Bettie was friendly with. Everyone else shunned her because of her temper and nastiness.

Auntie was all dressed up in a long floral print dress with matching scarf, a white belt, and blue and white flat leather shoes. Miss Bonnie greeted us at the door wearing a dark beige dress and light beige sandals. She looked really pretty and had a welcoming smile.

"Miss Bettie, Tony, how are ya? C'mon in and have a seat. I was just finishing fixin' dinna. Miss Bettie, can I fix ya a plate?"

"No, baby. Ya go head on an' eat yer dinna."

"Somethin' ta drank, what wouldya like?"

"A glass of ice wada be nice," said Auntie.

Miss Bonnie fixed her a large glass and they both sat down at the kitchen table. I quietly went over to a corner and sat down on the floor.

"Tony," Miss Bonnie said, "would ya like some dinna? I got fried chicken, green beans, mashed potatoes and my special cornbread. For dessert I got hot apple pie topped with vanilla ice cream, and a cold soft drink."

I looked over at Auntie for permission, and, of course, she gave me the evil eye. No way could I accept that wonderful dinner. I knew the repercussions.

"No, ma'am, Miss Bonnie," I said nervously.

"Are ya sure? Miss Bettie, can I make him a plate?"

"No! He all righ'. Dat boy don' need nothin'."

Then Miss Bonnie asked me why I was sitting in the corner. "You look so nice all dressed up," she said. "Come over here an' sit at da table wit us."

I thanked her and sat at the table as far away from Auntie as possible after getting her permission. Miss Bonnie went into her den and wheeled out the television set that was on a stand. She plugged it in, turned it on, and then fixed herself a dinner plate of food.

"The speech is gonna start in a few minutes," she said as she began to eat. "Miss Bettie, I saw ya in church Sunday. I guess ya are dere every Sunday but, I been missin' a lot. I wish I could be more like ya."

"Thank ya, baby," Auntie said. "God our savior. Dis boy need ta find God. He got da devil in him."

"No, Miss Bettie. Tony's a good boy."

"Ya don't know him like I do. He worthless!"

"Ah, Miss Bettie, ya really don't mean dat."

I sat with my head down, listening to the conversation, hungry and anxious. Out of the corner of my eye I couldn't resist watching our neighbor eat her meal. The smell was delicious and I was probably drooling.

"Oh, Dr. King is on!" Miss Bonnie said rapturously.

We all turned compellingly toward the television set. Auntie Bettie and Miss Bonnie were delighted and I wonder now, many years later, if they had a feeling that this particular speech was going to be an extremely important one as they both paid close attention. I sensed the tension in the air, but all I remember was of being proud that this African-Ameri-

Miss Bonnie, 1997

can man's speech was being nationally televised just like a famous Caucasian man's would be.

It was Wednesday, April 3, 1968, and Dr. King was at the Mason Temple in Memphis. A Baptist pastor in Montgomery, Alabama, and winner of the Nobel Peace Prize, he'd become a civil rights activist and world leader, traveling around America to encourage African-Americans to peacefully protest the current injustice. His audience that night was a group of sanitation workers who were on strike. They were all standing, listening to him intently. Dr. King took to the podium and delivered the speech that was heard around the world, "I've been to the mountaintop"

As an eleven year old I couldn't fully grasp the magnitude of the speech or the situation that was unfolding throughout the country but his powerful message left an indelible impression on me. The next evening, Thursday, April 4, 1968, Dr. King was assassinated. He was 39 years old.

CHAPTER 11

I t was great day at school when our teacher surprised us and took the class to the local public library. I was amazed to see all the stacks of books and shelves of magazines. I picked up a TIME magazine when I saw that it had a huge African-American man, a boxer, on the cover. It was someone I'd never heard of, Muhammad Ali. He was in his prime and winning all his fights. I thought he was the handsomest man I'd ever seen. I never forgot that cover. Many years later, I realized it showed how perfectly his build was in the picture, taken after he'd won the World Heavyweight Championship title. He was wearing the famous green leather belt around his waist with its massive gold circular buckle. I stared at that magazine cover, then read the article inside the best I could. I put the magazine down and we left, after a while I kind of forgot about him.

When I was 13 years of age Auntie Bettie received a letter from her daughter. Alberta rarely wrote and hardly ever phoned her mom. I can remember Auntie receiving a letter only once before, and I'd overheard a couple of phone calls from Miss Bonnie's house to let Auntie know Alberta was coming for a visit. I didn't care what the letter said. It had nothing to do with my harsh life. But this time I was wrong. So wrong, it would lead to the circumstances that would change my life.

"Tony, git yer butt in here!" Auntie shouted to me from the back door of the shack. I was sitting on a small, low stool in the yard watching the chickens run around. I wasn't allowed in the house on weekends except to change into my Sunday clothes for church. I spent both days outside chopping firewood or collecting eggs and playing pretend games with myself.

"Yes, ma'am."

I ran into the house as fast as possible. Auntie would always hit me if I didn't come right away. She put the letter in my hand.

"Read it!" She commanded.

She didn't read well, and her eyesight was beginning to fade at that time. No one in our community could afford to get their eyesight checked like regular folks, and over time some of them ultimately went blind. I began reading Alberta's letter out loud.

"Dear Mama, I thank it time foe ya an' Tony ta move ta St. Louis an' live wit me. Ya is gettin' older. I'm concerned bout yer health. I worry a lot bout ya an' Tony. Memphis is too far foe me ta get der in time if ya needed me. I thank Tony will like it here. The junior high skool is very nice an' new, it is a state of da art facility."

My heart leapt when Auntie, after listening to me read the letter, said, "I gonna call yer Uncle Rabbit ta help move us. He work down der at da U-Haul place." She gripped my shoulder hard and shook it. "Well boy, don' jes' stand der. Ya better start gittin' yer thangs tagethe' now cuz I know how slow ya is ta git anythin' done round here."

"I will, I will! I so excited bout movin' ta St. Louis."

Auntie, of course, immediately crushed my enthusiasm by saying, "Jes' cuz we movin' up der don' change a thang. Ya betta remember I still in charge. My doughter cain't control me. I whip her ass if she git outta line."

A few days later we were ready for Uncle Rabbit, as we called him, to drive us in the U-Haul to St Louis, a major city 300 miles north of Memphis. Auntie sold as many of the farm animals as she could. She tried to sell the furniture, too, but it was in such awful shape no one wanted it so it was left in the shack. She found a couple of battered old suitcases at the thrift store for our things. That was one of the most fun-filled days of my young life. It was great to see Uncle Rabbit. His real name was Odell, but everyone called him Rabbit. He was a really cool guy, every now and then he would visit us at the shack. We talked a lot during the trip and I was blissful, wide-eyed, staring out the window watching the towns go by. Auntie kept quiet. Perhaps, she was feeling apprehensive about the move.

Alberta's two-story house was like a mansion to me. It was in the city on a nice two-way street, and had three bedrooms in addition to a living room, a kitchen, a den, and two bathrooms. There was none of the squalor I had gotten used to back in Memphis. I remember being so impressed with everything and thinking, *Wow! It's so neat and beautiful!* It became my job every Saturday to clean it thoroughly to keep it that way.

I entered Normandy Junior High School in St. Louis in 1970. I really felt out of place, most of all for my deep Southern accent. The students and teachers spoke regular English, while my dialect sounded almost like a foreign language to some of them. Some of the kids mimicked my speech and made fun of me as I was subjected to a lot of teasing and even bullying. I was naturally shy because of my isolated upbringing and the fact that many Southerners are reserved, unlike the Midwesterners I was now among. Back in Memphis all the kids at my old school spoke the way I did. But junior high in St. Louis was a different environment and culture altogether. Moreover, half of the school kids at my new school were Caucasian. I'd never been around so many Caucasian kids before. The backwoods of Memphis was the real Deep South, and all of us in the community and at my grade school, Weaver Elementary, were African-American.

Amazingly, when I finally settled in at the St. Louis school, most of my best friends were white. I'd go to their homes and feel completely comfortable. No one used racial slurs. We all got along; looking back it was such a peaceful time except for being teased for the way I spoke. I determined to change my accent by copying their English. I worked hard at practicing the way my classmates said the words as I walked back home from school each day. Fortunately, I was able to shed my accent quite easily while I still spoke to Auntie Bettie and Alberta the way I always had. I knew my Auntie would wonder what was going on if I let her hear my new way of speaking, and she'd probably beat the living daylights out of me for being what African-Americans called "uppity."

Our lives settled into a routine that still included both Auntie Bettie and Alberta drinking heavily, and me getting a whipping. One Saturday morning I went into the kitchen where Auntie was sitting at the kitchen table watching her favorite television show. I felt very uneasy when I asked her if I could go to the football game if I got through my cleaning chores early.

"No," she said, as I expected. "Ya gotta clean dis house."

I then made the mistake of complaining aloud, "I never get to do anything. I can't wait until I'm old enough to move out."

The comment set Auntie Bettie on fire. She jumped out of her chair and came rushing at me, knocking me down the basement stairs. I laid there, dizzy. I heard her come thumping down the stairs and then I felt a gun pressed to my forehead. "Jes cuz ya foeteen ya thank yer grown? Ya thank yer a big main now? Ya wanna start challengin' me, disrespectin' me in my own damn house? Answer me, boy!"

Terror-stricken, I murmured, "No, ma'am." I knew she was crazy enough to pull the trigger.

"I cain't fuckin' hear ya."

"No, ma'am," I said louder.

"I gonna put a bullet in yer head an' bury yer ass in da back yard." Her words came out like the hiss of a snake. "Do ya unnerstan'?"

"Yes ma'am! Yes ma'am."

"Now git yer skinny ugly ass up an' if dis house ain't clean ta my likin' ya gonna do it all over gain. An' ya ain't gittin' nothin' ta eat taday neither."

I finished my chores and escaped into the basement like I'd always done when I came home from school or needed to get away from Auntie Bettie's relentless wrath. Down there I had a desk in a corner. It was kind of dark with not much light. During the hot, blistering summers it was the coolest place in the house. I'd sit there and daydream. It felt like I was living in a fantasy world, imagining I was in a faraway place called California. I had a little transistor radio and it was always playing songs about how great California was. I'd listen, dream, and doodle, drawing people and cars. I loved little hot-rod racers, and I came up with some pretty good sketches.

CHAPTER 12

One day I was walking home from hanging out at the park when I saw in the distance a long, black limousine pull up to the entrance of a high school down the street. The limousine had a full police escort. *Wow! Must be some high-up government official*, I thought, *or surely it had to be the President of the United States!* The driver parked, got out, and opened the door to the back seat. Out stepped Muhammad Ali. He was wearing a dark blue suit. He looked exactly like the superhero I'd seen on the magazine cover in the library. Here was my favorite boxer forever! I ran as fast as I could to the limo and stood in front of him in awe, staring up. I'm sure my eyes were as big as the sky. You could see the muscles rippling under his silk jacket. I'd never seen anyone look like that, and here he was in real life. I managed to say, "Sir! Sir! Can I shake your hand?"

He gave me a big smile and enveloped my hand in his massive one, "Wow, oh my God, this is so cool. Unbelievable!"

The champ let go of my hand, smiled again, and started to walk really fast to the school entrance. I ran along beside him, reaching up and touching his shoulder just before he entered.

At that moment, when I touched him, I had an epiphany. I somehow believed that I was an old soul. I have always felt that our lives are planned before we are born, that a path is already laid out for us and destiny brings people to us that will have an impact. I had never known there was a boxer like Muhammad

Ali. I didn't follow anything about the boxing world until I read that TIME article. But I knew that something earth-shaking had just happened to me. I felt that this moment foretold something about my future, that Muhammad Ali would completely change the direction of my life. This fateful encounter would inspire me sooner than later to get involved in sports.

The next day I saw my best friend, Scott Harper, in the school cafeteria, and told him about meeting Ali. He couldn't believe it.

"For real! Wow!" He said. "I can't believe you saw Muhammad Ali here in St. Louis. That's awesome, man. You met the heavyweight champion of the world, bro, the greatest of all time."

"So cool, right?" I replied, still extremely happy and amazed. "Man, dude! Meeting him got me so excited, I am going to try out for some sports. I don't know which one yet. I wasn't allowed to play any sports growing up. I was too busy trying to figure out how to survive another day. I can't really see myself boxing, though."

"You're really strong. Why don't you try out for the wrestling team?" Scott said.

Scott was right, I was very strong for my size. Maybe it's because of my hard life growing up. It could have been from my dad too, as he had pretty good genetics.

By this time my upper body had filled out, especially my chest and arms, although my legs were strong but lacked muscle development. Even so, I decided to try out for the team.

Two weeks later I came across Scott at his locker. "Hey, Scott, I made it! I made the wrestling team!" I exclaimed, barely able to contain my enthusiasm.

"That's awesome, bro," he replied, with a big smile as we high-fived each other.

"Yeah, it's so cool, right!" I said. "I've got practice before and after school. We'll be going to other schools to compete against their squads. Hey, I've got to get to class, let's talk later."

I determined to work hard and to become the best wrestler on the team. Our training consisted mostly of practicing on the mats, weight lifting, and rope climbing. I hated the weight-lifting at first but after a while I began exerting myself more and more and seeing how much I could lift. Lifting weights is quantitative and became a great way for me to rid myself of stress. Still being denied breakfast at home by my Auntie, one of my wrestling teammate's mom were so kind, she would send me breakfast daily to school.

I got up extra early to make the morning practice. As I left for school that day I felt as if I was on cloud nine. My self-confidence soared after being picked by the wrestling coach, Bob Camp. He was in his early 40s, with a muscular build, a former wrestling champion, and had a great personality. This was the first time I was actually part of a team. Maybe I could really make something of myself. I thought back to the epiphany I had after meeting world boxing champion Muhammad Ali. I learned all about his life after that day and read everything about him I could find in the school library. My admiration for this grand guy was boundless and I followed the news of his career as much as possible. I was grateful to him for inspiring me to try out for wrestling. Even though I was over-joyed about making the team, it didn't make up for my wretched home life though. I'd usually sit in class and stare unfocused out the window or just into space. I couldn't concentrate on my lessons and eventually the teachers became concerned enough to take action.

"Tony," the teacher called out to me one day in class. "Please come up front."

"Yes, ma'am."

I made my way slowly to her desk, wondering but not really caring what the problem was.

"I'm sending you down to the counselor's office," she said.

"Don't be alarmed. Everything is fine."

"Did I do something wrong, ma'am?"

"No, everything is going to be just fine. The counselor would like to speak with you. Don't worry, you'll be okay."

CHAPTER 13

Mr. Neely was the high school counselor. He was a kindly man, African-American, and in his 40s. He was very calm and serious when I walked into his office. It was well known among the students that he was passionate about the well-being and safety of the students at our school as well as for all children in general.

"My teacher sent me down here," I said. "She said you wanted to see me."

"Yes. You're Tony, right?"

After I said I was, Mr. Neely told me to take a seat and began to tell me the reason I had been asked to come in.

"You're here because I've been receiving reports from your teachers that something could be amiss. The main report is that you aren't focused on your studies. You seem aloof and greatly withdrawn, spending most of your time staring into space. Collectively, we feel that you're showing signs of suicidal behavior."

When he said that my jaw dropped open. Really? Was that how I appeared to the teachers? How did they know? I felt gloomy most of the time because of my sad life, and thoughts of taking my life had repeatedly entered my mind. It seemed to be my only escape. Many times over the years I had wished I was dead. I guess my lack of attention in class and low grades were among the typical symptoms students showed that warned the staff that they could be on the edge of being suicidal.

As I turned over Mr. Neely's words in my mind, he went on to say, "We find that to be alarming. I just want you to know we are here to help and support our kids with personal issues that otherwise wouldn't have anywhere to go for help. I realize this could be a little uncomfortable but you have no reason to be shy or frightened. Please, Tony, feel free to express anything you might be going through."

I sat there, speechless. This was the first time anyone in authority had ever offered to help me. After some hesitation I said, "Ah…this is not easy for me, 'cause I've never told anyone about my life."

"Excuse me, where're you from? I can detect you have a bit of an accent." While I'd been working hard to get rid of my Southern accent, there were still traces of it left and every now and then I'd slip back into it, especially when I was nervous.

"Memphis," I said. "Sir, I've been working hard to lose it. All of the other kids are making fun of me with the way I talk."

Mr. Neely smiled caringly at me. "Don't worry, you're doing just fine. So, how long have you been in St. Louis?"

"Three years, sir."

"Please continue, as you were saying."

I was so shy and very reluctant to describe what I had been experiencing, but here was my chance to confide in someone that had the capability to intervene, and who could save me from my misery. I just hoped he believed me.

"I've never told anyone because it's painful and embarrassing," I said. "I don't want anyone to know. My home life has gotten worse over the last few years. It began when my mom and dad divorced when I was a baby. My dad took me to live with my great-auntie. She's always been physically abusive. And lately she has taken to threatening me with a gun. I am so afraid of her. She's crazy."

Mr. Neely looked shocked as I spoke. "This is unthinkable," he said, shaking his head. "How often does the abuse occur?"

"Almost daily. It's all I've ever known. It's been a living hell with no escape. I tried running away many times and hiding with neighbors but she always found me. I have never been allowed to have any friends, and after school I have to go straight home. Sir, you don't understand. I'm so scared right now, I'm trembling inside. If she knew I was in here talking to you she would literally torture me to death. Ya gotta help me. I cain't take it anymore." I began to cry. I was choked up but still managed to say, undoubtedly confirming his suspicion that I could be suicidal, "I wish I could just fly away. I feel like I don't want to live anymore."

He took out his handkerchief and gave it to me. "Please don't cry, son. Try to calm down. It's going to be all right. I completely understand what you're going through. We will definitely help you. We'll take this matter very seriously. I want to assure you you're going to be safe. First, though, I have to contact the State of Missouri for assistance and follow the proper protocol to have you removed from the home through the courts."

"Sir, you don't know who you're dealing with. She's a mean old lady that's fearful of no one. She has a shotgun and a handgun, too."

"Don't worry. You will become a ward of the state. There is nothing she can do to harm you anymore. We'll have a couple of fully trained police officers that have dealt with situations of this nature before at your home to make certain everything goes smoothly. Until then, try to continue your daily life as normal."

Normal? I'd hoped things would change when we came to live with Alberta, but as soon as she left the house to go to work,

Auntie Bettie would be back to her old self, except worse. I no longer had to go into the woods to find a tree switch for a beating because the belt left deeper wounds.

"Mr. Neely, thank you, sir. No one has ever tried to help me before. I've never been free. I can't imagine what it's like!"

"You're welcome, young man. This isn't down South, you know. This is the State of Missouri. We don't tolerate this type of behavior. It's our responsibility to protect our innocent children."

He stood up, shook my hand, and patted me on the back when I left his office. As I walked home, I hardly dared hope I could get away from Auntie. She had dominated my life. Could it be true that Mr. Neely was able to change all that?

CHAPTER 14

A few weeks later I heard a car approaching our house. Alberta had already left for work. I looked out the window and saw a police car. Two officers got out and knocked on the door. My heart felt as if it was going to stop. Were they coming to take me out of this hellhole? I began to shiver with fear because I knew how my Auntie Bettie would react.

"Who is it?" Auntie shouted.

"Police, ma'am. Please open the door."

When she did, blocking it as much as possible with her massive body, she was asked, "Miss. Pearson?"

"Yes. How can I help ya?"

"We're here to serve you with a court order allowing us to remove Tony Pearson from this residence." One of the officers held up a sheet of paper. "We want to ensure that the young man can gather his belongings safely. We must ask you to step aside."

The officers entered and handed a court order to Auntie Bettie. She took it, then flung it to the floor. I was ready to rush out the back door if things got ugly but with two officers in the house I figured maybe for once Auntie would hold back her temper. Not a chance. She stood facing them with hostility, hands on her hips, challenging the officers.

"I don't know what dat boy told ya," she yelled, almost

spitting in their faces, "but it all a pack o' lies. Dat's all dat boy do, is lie. Damn it, hurry up, an' git him outta here, befoe I kill 'em."

The police officer stepped back from her aggressive move. I saw him glance towards the shotgun Auntie kept behind the door like she had in Memphis. It was in full sight. He signaled to the other officer, who went over to stand in front of it so she couldn't reach it.

"Miss. Pearson, I would advise you to refrain from speaking. We don't want to make this situation any more tense for the child than it already is."

Auntie wasn't used to being told what to do by anyone other than my dad. As I watched the officer and Auntie confronting each other, I had no idea how this was going to play out. She was an extremely tough woman and I was very fearful that she might bring out the pistol she kept in her apron pocket.

She started to come towards me in a threatening way and I prepared to try to slip past her, but before she could get any closer to where I stood with my back pressed against the wall one of the officers blocked her way.

"Miss. Pearson, I'm ordering you not to take another step forward toward the child. Now get back or I'll be forced to arrest you. We have the court order, and you must obey it."

She turned to the officer and pushed him with her muscular arms. He staggered back, surprised at her strength, and a scuffle ensued, with her screaming like a mad woman. It took both officers to subdue her and hold her against the front door. I was told to get my things. With practically no possessions aside from my clothes and schoolbooks, it took me about ten minutes to gather them up and stuff them into my little old suitcase. My heart was pounding, this time with happiness. I couldn't believe my years-long nightmare was truly coming to an end.

"Sir," I said to one of the officers, "I'm ready."

The officers had to forcibly move Auntie Bettie away from the door, and wished her a good day. I knew Auntie must have been glaring at me with hatred as I passed her while the officers escorted me out, but I didn't even glance back at her as I went through the door.

One of the officers took my suitcase and put it in the trunk of the police car, then opened the back door for me to get in. I guessed the neighbors would be wondering what was going on as we drove past their homes. Maybe they thought I'd been arrested!

As we left, I couldn't help but wonder how my Auntie Bettie could be such a God-fearing woman who went to the Baptist church every Sunday and listened to Gospel music, and yet treated a young child – me – with such brutality.

I couldn't remember the last time I'd ridden in a car. We always took a bus or walked where we needed to go. Sitting in the police car was a new sensation. I ran my hand over the leather seats, enjoyed the air conditioning, and listened to the police radio and the calls that came in. There was a burglary going on downtown St. Louis, and a kid had gone missing. I had no idea where I was being taken but it didn't matter. Anywhere but with my Auntie Bettie would be grand.

The car pulled up in front of a two-story building on the outskirts of St. Louis.

It looked like kind of an old institution, with two of the window panes cracked. It was a state group home. One of the officers took me inside to the reception desk, where I was registered. The officer said goodbye and wished me good luck. A counselor introduced himself and took me up two flights of stairs and into a dorm with about ten single beds, like cots. I was told which one was mine, and given a locker for my stuff. Then he showed me the cafeteria, and finally the recreation room where a group of kids was watching a baseball game on television. The sofas and chairs looked old and battered and the bare floor was all scratched up. But, hey, I was out of Auntie Bettie's life, and a new one for me was beginning. Yet, would I be wrong again?

CHAPTER 15

A couple of weeks later, on a Sunday afternoon, I received a phone call at the home's front desk. By now I'd settled in, but it was nothing like I'd expected. The kids were rowdy, boasted about the crimes they'd committed, and, worst of all, had fistfights day and night. There was very little supervision, and the inmates were running the prison. Nighttime brought out more bullying, and several times I was dragged out of bed and told to fight.

I was in the recreation room when the counselor found me and said there was a phone call at the front desk. He told me that I was to make it quick to keep the line open. I went out to the desk in the hall and picked up the receiver.

"Hey, bro. What's up?" Said Scott.

"Hey, man, what's going on?" I replied.

"How's it going down there?" Scott asked.

I leaned over the front desk and half-covered the mouthpiece with my hand so no one could hear me. I felt it was time to tell someone about the conditions at this group home, and Scott was the person I trusted the most to disclose it to.

"Man, it's crazy in this place. It's dangerous. There's about thirty boys living here and I think most of them have been involved in some sort of crime. I spend most of my nights in the dorm fighting, trying to defend myself. They force everyone to put on boxing gloves and take turns fighting each other. They think it's fun but a lot of kids have been getting hurt pretty badly. If you don't fight back they all jump you."

"Wow!" Scott said. "That's awful. Doesn't the staff try to stop it?"

"No, they don't care. The other night a boy knocked out another kid and everyone began laughing. He hit his head really hard on the floor. It's a nightmare. But I heard
this place might be closing. I don't know what I'm going to do, or where I'll live, if it does."

"Hey, man, that's why I'm calling. Somehow I just knew it couldn't be good there so I was telling my mom about your problem and she said she would adopt you."

"What? Adopt me? Are you sure!" I couldn't believe my ears. I was completely stunned.

"Yes. She means it. You can come and live with us."

"Aw, man." I told Scott how excited I was at his mother's generosity. "That's so cool. Your mom is the best."

Her name was a somewhat peculiar one, Madir, and she made good on her word. At age 16 I was legally adopted by the Harper family and was given the spare bedroom.

Petite, in her late-50s, kindly, and easy-going, Madir and Scott welcomed me with open arms. It was the first time I was part of a real family. I could hardly believe my luck.

CHAPTER 16

O ne morning when Madir was making breakfast, she asked why I had been leaving to go to school so early for the past few weeks.

"I have wrestling practice before class. I've been doing really well in my matches. I won the last two," I said proudly, thinking she'd congratulate me.

"Tony, I don't want to hear anything about wrestling," she said sternly. "I don't know why you want to do that. Instead of spending all your time up there at the school, you should be going out looking for a job. You're old enough to find something. You boys are going to eat me out of a house and home." She had a serious expression as she said it, and I knew she was right. Scott worked with his dad in his spare time and I decided I'd check out local places where I could work.

I'd been living with the Harper's for a year and a half and at age 18 I was looking forward to my next birthday and graduation. An idea had been growing in my mind and I wanted to talk it over with Scott. Before I could, though, disaster struck. I came home from school limping terribly. The pain was almost unbearable and I winced as I sat down in the living room where Madir was watching the news on television.

"What happened to you?" Her voice was full of concern.

"I injured my knee during a match. The coach, Mr. Camp,

rushed me to the doctor, who said I was going to need surgery. He says my wrestling days are over."

"Oh, my God," said Madir. "I told you that you shouldn't be wrestling. Now look what happened. You boys never listen. Well, go in the kitchen and make me a drink, and light me a cigarette from the stove. I'm so sick and tired of you both and your shenanigans. I'll be glad when you two are old enough to move out."

"Yes, ma'am," I said, hobbling into the kitchen.

I was feeling really down and disappointed. I'd been so happy to be on a sports team. I was in shock when I injured my knee. Things were going well for me during the match and I was getting the better of my opponent. Then, he made at once an unexpected move and all I could hear was my knee ripping apart.

A day later surgery was performed on my knee by Dr. Jenkins, a well-known surgeon. The next day, as I lay in the hospital bed, he came to check up on me.

"Mr. Pearson," he said, "I want you to know that the surgery went well but we'll need to keep you here for another week or so for further observation. It's going to take three to four months for the knee to fully heal. I hate to be the bearer of bad news, but I advise you to stop wrestling. Your athletic career is over, I'm sorry to say. You had multiple tears and your knee will never be the same."

I was devastated. I had hoped against hope that my knee would be repaired enough for me to rejoin the team, but Dr. Jenkins' news was a death knell. The thought of Muhammad Ali was still in my mind, and maybe I could have made wrestling my career. Well, that'd been confirmed - it was over, for sure.

"I recommend you find a gym," he said, "and after the healing process is complete, figure out how to rehab the knee yourself. It could be a long road."

I said sadly, "thank you, doctor."

After he left, I lay there with my eyes closed, feeling like my life had ended.

My dream of becoming an athlete had just gone up in smoke. As I contemplated my future, the nurse came back into the room and touched my shoulder.

"Excuse me, Mr. Pearson. You have a visitor outside. She says she's your sister Carolyn."

Carolyn! I pushed myself into a sitting position. How did she manage to find me? It seemed like a miracle. Carolyn was older than me and she'd always looked out for me. "Yes, let her in, please!"

Seconds later, Carolyn rushed into the room calling my name. Her smile was so wide, her eyes shining with such joy. I felt really grateful for having this wonderful sister.

"Hi, little brother. How're you doing? I heard what happened." She gave me a big hug.

"Hey, sis! What's up? I'm not doing too good as you can tell. How did you know I was here?"

She just smiled. "I told you, little brother, I can track you down anywhere. I knew you were at Auntie Bettie's in Memphis, and that you'd moved to live with Alberta in St. Louis. Three years later I moved here, too. I lived with Auntie Bettie for a while until she asked me to leave. So then, I moved in with my friend Patty and her mom."

"Oh yeah, I remember them, they used to live down the street from Auntie Bettie."

"So, what's with the knee?" She asked.

"I'm on the wrestling team at school, and during one of the matches I had a leg in and the other guy sat out the wrong way and twisted it. It was horrible, you could hear the ligaments tearing. The pain almost made me pass out."

"Sounds like you have a long recovery ahead. Did they

give you something for the pain?"

"Yeah, but they don't help much. I leave here in another week, and they said I'd be on crutches for six weeks. What's been happening with you?"

"Still working in the restaurant, putting in a lot of hours, and, of course having a little fun." She responded.

"I won't be having any fun for a while. I love wrestling, but the doctor thinks my career is over before it even started."

Carolyn said she been trying to get over to the Harper's house but was so busy at work lately. She asked how it was going there for me.

"It's going good, Madir is really nice… well, when she's not drinking. She adopted me almost three months ago."

"Really? That's great," said Carolyn, not sounding surprised. She always rolled with the punches. "I'll definitely have to meet her. We'll get together when you're feeling better. Now, little brother, I have to get back to work. Here's my phone number."

The doctor was right. It took a full four months for the knee to recover. I knew wrestling was out but I still wanted to be a professional athlete. The future was bleak. What will I do with my life now? Then, a couple of months later while watching television after school one day with Scott, a commercial came on that seemed to answer my question.

CHAPTER 17

"The Few. The Proud. The Marines. Join today!"

When the Marine Corps commercial began with its stirring music and videos of the Marines doing exciting things, it caught my full attention. I listened to the guy in uniform describing how great the service was, what it meant to be a Marine, and the many benefits it granted to recruits.

"Look at that!" I said to Scott. "You get housing, a salary and career training. That's it! I'm going to join the Marines."

"Man, you're crazy." Scott said.

"No, I'm serious. Being a Marine means you'll be defending your country. What's more rewarding than that? It's something you can always be proud of. Plus, maybe I'll be stationed in Southern California. I've always felt drawn to that place. I need to get out of here. What kind of future do I have other than drugs and crime?" Scott kind of rolled his eyes and shook his head at my harsh words.

"I don't know, man. That sounds a little extreme to me. Are you sure?"

"Yeah, I'm sure. I'm old enough now. I'm going to go down to the recruiting office first thing tomorrow morning."

The next morning I woke up inspired and kept my word. Having called and got their address, I made an appointment for the afternoon. I was instructed to wear appropriate clothing for a physical exam. I arrived at the recruiting office in shorts, a T-shirt, and sneakers. The officer in charge, a Caucasian in his mid-30s, was tall, blonde, well-built, and had a deep voice with a serious demeanor.

"So," he said, looking me up and down. "You want to be a Marine? How old are you?"

"Yes, sir." I replied. "I just turned eighteen, sir."

"To become a Marine," he said, "requires a great deal of fortitude and discipline. I don't know if you have what it takes to become a Marine, son, but we'll see. First, we'll have to put you through a physical exam. If you pass, you'll have to come back tomorrow and take a written test."

"Yes, sir."

"So, let's get started. First thing I want you to do is get down and give me fifteen military style pushups. On your toes, body in a straight line. Hands positioned shoulder-width apart."

"Okay."

"That's sir to you, son," he barked.

"Yes, sir. Sir!"

"That's more like it."

I performed a set of 15 pushups.

"Next, give me a set of twenty pull-ups."

As I got almost through them he began counting. "Eighteen…nineteen…twenty. You're doing all right so far. The last exercise is called a duck walk. I want to see you duck walk across the room and back."

I knew what a duck walk was. I got into a deep squat position with my legs wider than my hips and my weight on my heels. My hands were clasped together at my chest to keep my balance. I pulled in my abdominal muscles, but as I began walking forward I winced in pain.

"Ouch! It's my knee, sir. Every time I try to walk like that I'm getting a real sharp pain in my right knee."

"Looks like you've got a bum knee there. What happened?" I told him about the injury I got during the wrestling match.

The officer looked at me with sympathy. "Son, you seem to be in great shape except for that knee. It looks pretty torn up to me. You can't run ten miles on that knee. Furthermore, it's impossible for you to go into hand-to-hand combat. That's a problem for the Marine Corps. I'm sorry, son, you don't qualify. We're looking for healthy bodies. We don't need a liability on our hands. I'm going to have to flunk you."

I was heartbroken at what he'd said. Joining the Marines had seemed like the perfect answer to my prayers.

"Sir! Please, sir. What if I waited six months, maybe then it'll be better."

"Sorry," he said, shaking his head. "I've made my decision. The Marine Corps isn't for you."

I dropped my head as I headed toward the exit. "Don't be down on yourself," he said strongly. "Keep your head up. Stay positive. Good things are in your future."

Disappointed, I left his office after thanking him, and went back to the Harper's house.

CHAPTER 18

My mind was still filled with the dream of moving out West to California, I light-heartedly read all the hype of how no one had a care in the world in the Golden State. I probably brainwashed myself into thinking how incredible it would be to go out there. But then, I just blocked it out of my mind thinking it was impossible. Plus, I needed to graduate first.

I decided to intensify my efforts to rehab my knee and, of course, targeting the rest of my muscle groups. I trained hard daily, as it was a lot of fun.

Coach Camp came into the weight room at school one day where I was working out. In the middle of a bench press I got stuck and he rushed over to help me. After I completed the set he asked how my training was going.

High school, 19 years old

"It's coming along," I said. "It's going good. I've gotten a lot stronger and I'm gaining some solid muscle."

"I can see, that's great. How many days are you working out?" He asked.

"Umm, I'm here every day. I love lifting."

"Who's helping you with your training?"

"No one," I said. "I train my whole body every day myself."

In fact, I saw how fast my body was changing. There were muscles beginning to develop where I'd never seen any before or even knew I had. Mr. Camp seemed to be thinking for a moment.

"I believe you have the potential to build a great physique," Coach said. "Would you like to go to a real gym? I'm going there tomorrow."

"Yes sir! I can't wait!" Aside from his exciting offer, the coach's remarks surprised me. I had to pinch myself. I couldn't believe what he'd said. This was like a dream come true. He'd been around bodybuilders, and for him to say he thought I had the potential was music to my ears.

CHAPTER 19

George Turner's gym in Clayton, on the border of St. Louis, was to become as legendary and as revered as Gold's Gym in Venice, California, where he had trained years earlier. He was an avid amateur bodybuilder and had entered a few contests, but the gym was his life and he was there every day. The gym was home to professional bodybuilders, among them Ken Waller, Dave Johns, and Samir Bannout, and later on, the Enigma, twice National Champion Phil Williams. It was always full of hopeful athletes working out. George knew the best techniques. If someone was doing lifts or whatever incorrectly, he would tell him to either follow the right technique or "get the fuck out of my gym!"

He wrote a series of articles for *Muscle Builder and Power* magazine and we all read them ardently. I still have one George wrote on drugs, specifically steroids, and how detrimental they were because bodybuilders needed to learn how their bodies reacted to hard work. If we took drugs, he wrote, it would change and distort the normal response to training and nutrition. In high school, I'd never taken drugs, not at all been tempted to, either. However, I'm sure, it had its percentage of kids who did. But my focus was initially on learning how to fit in, work out, and be the best wrestler on our squad. The same went for bodybuilding. I learned far more from George Turner than how to train my muscles correctly. I learned how to mentally focus on a particular muscle group during an exercise. And he advised me on nutrition. But most importantly, he taught me about life in general. He would later become more like a father figure to me.

Mr. Camp took me to Turner's gym. I was in heaven – it was a brand new gym, a real gym, huge and cavernous, with all new equipment and weights, everything beyond imagination for an 18 year old kid from the backwoods of Tennessee.

I spent three hours training that first day, and unbeknownst to me, I was being watched by George the entire time. Suddenly, George came over to me and shouted. "What the fuck you think you're doing? You can't train for three damn hours. Get in my office!"

Scared and confused, I went into George's office. "Did I do something wrong, sir?" I stammered, unsure of what was to come.

George looked right at me, and said "I'm going to train you. Be here at 6pm tomorrow and don't be late. Now get the hell out of here, I'm busy."

I rushed home to tell Scott the good news. "Scott! Hey man, you won't believe what happened today. Mr. Camp, you know, my wrestling coach, took me to George Turner's gym. Man, it's huge! Everything is brand new, it smells like new, too, it just opened a few weeks ago. It's George Turner's Gym! I was in the middle of doing the same work out there as I did at school, and the owner comes over and offers to train me. Scott, George Turner is going to be my trainer!"

Scott, deeply engrossed in a basketball game on TV, appeared not to hear me, so I repeated, "Scott!! Did you hear what I just said? He's going to TRAIN me. Remember a few weeks ago when I was watching Wide World of Sports and I saw Arnold Schwarzenegger and this other guy, Robby Robinson. And Arnold won Mr. Olympia. Remember?"

Scott finally responded, "I hear, bro. I remember."

"So maybe with a trainer I could look like those guys," I said. "Mr. Camp thinks I've got potential. I'm so excited. This is the best day of my life!"

"Cool. That's great! I know you can do it, man." Scott replied.

The next evening, my education with George began. I arrived promptly at 6pm, wearing a pair of old sweat pants, a T-shirt, and run-down sneakers without shoelaces. It sure wasn't great gear but it was all I had. I didn't care if I was the worst-dressed member there.

"Let's get started, kid. We're going to build you a foundation starting with those bird legs. You'll be doing squats of ten sets of ten reps Monday, Wednesday, and Friday. I also want the same amount of sets and reps on pull-ups on Tuesday, Thursday, and Saturday. That's all you're going to do. I don't want to see you doing anything else till I tell you. Is that understood?"

"Yes, sir."

"What did you eat today?" He asked.

"I had some Wheaties this morning." I said shyly.

"And what the hell do you think you're going to build with that? You might as well tear up the box and eat it. Hell, with that outfit you're wearing I can tell you ain't got no money. Every time you finish your workout here I want you to go next door to the restaurant and order a pound of beef and a baked potato. Tell them to put it on my bill."

"Yes, sir. Thank you, sir." I was almost unable to speak. What a great dinner every night!

Then he told me I was to clean the gym four days a week.

"And I don't mean a half-ass job," he said. "Every inch of this place better be spotless."

I assured him it would be.

He was kind of intimidating because of his critiques, but I have never forgotten the day he came up to me at the gym when I was doing deadlifts, with his permission, of course. He stood in front of me and said, "You've got potential, kid. I think I can make you a champion!"

For a high school junior with a banged-up knee, barely weighing 140lbs., What George had said was amazing and in-spiring. He was the second person to tell me that I had talent and potential.

George's statement proved to be prophetic. But first I had a very long road to travel. Under his training I gained 25lbs., of muscle, and acquired unlimited determination. He spurred me on to workouts that were way beyond anything I'd have ever imagined. It was exhilarating. I had definitely been bitten with the bodybuilding bug and spent every extra hour I'd find at the gym.

CHAPTER 20

Three months into my training, George took me through a grueling leg workout. I'd already trained them on Monday and Wednesday. Training them on Fridays was always the toughest because they were completely exhausted but George couldn't care less. He never let up. I was to complete my usual ten sets of ten reps of squats increasing the weight per set up to 405lbs., By now, I couldn't have weighed more than 150lbs., I could tell he was trying to break me, but he didn't realize how tough and tenacious I was, something I'd learned as a child growing up as a way of survival. It seems that I'd been unknowingly and, surely, unwillingly conditioned myself along those lines during those tortured years at the hands of my Auntie. George was unwavering and he was often in a really bad mood. And could be unpleasantly critical. At such times, he threw the "fuck" word around like it was confetti. But I knew deep down he was a caring person. He just had a peculiar way of showing it.

"After three months of this shit, son," he said, "we've got to get to the next level with this little dance. This ain't where you sign up for a picnic. My grandmother can out-squat you. Get your belt on. For God's sakes, go find the fucking belt!"

As I was barely able to stand up to go get one of the gym's weightlifting belts, I said to George, "George, my legs are really sore. I can hardly walk." That was the wrong thing to say to

George.

He turned toward me, eyes ablaze, face drawn tight and red with anger, and let me have it with both barrels in front of the whole gym. "Excuse me!" He roared. "I think you've made a mistake. The daycare is two blocks over. This is the gym where men train. The girl's gym is down the fucking street. Maybe, you should get your ass down there. I think the aerobic classes just started."

I was humiliated. I hurried and got my belt on. To this day I am convinced this was part of George's plan to make sure that no matter what, you should always stay the course. Lesson learned.

As I continued training, still distressing from the embarrassment, music began playing loudly in the background. George jumped up from leaning on one of the weight machines as if he's ready to punch somebody. He began yelling at one of the members. "Hey, asshole, the one that brought your own fucking music today. Turn that damn noise off! I don't want to hear some asshole dude sounding like some girly-girl. You know music ain't allowed here. If it ever happens again, sunshine, you'll be the fuck out of here as quick as a rattlesnake!"

He turned back to me where I was at the rack loading up the bar by adding weights plates to each side, preparing for doing a set of squats. George began giving me instructions.

"Now get your butt under that bar. I want you to keep your head up. Look at that spot in the ceiling to help you focus. Now, slowly walk it back from the rack. I'll count the damn reps. You're not mounting a horse. You should know your feet should be shoulder width apart. You've got to get the first seven reps without locking out. Rest between the last three."

"Yes, sir," I said. I obeyed George's instructions and I began, quietly grunting at the effort. That resulted in more of his colorful language.

"Hey kid, you don't need to make so much noise. You're

waking up the neighbors. And I want a full squat, not that half-squat bullshit."

I completed all ten reps and replaced the bar on the rack, taking a minute or so to rest. Then I looked at George and said. "George, I'm ready."

"That's the fucking spirit," he replied. "The last set either makes or breaks you. Don't puss out. You have to show me you've got what it takes. I need you to get under that damn bar with some fire."

I took the bar off the rack and walked it back and got into position. I pushed myself extremely hard to finish the final set and heard George say, "That's the way to grind those bastards out. Now get next door and eat something."

After six months of intense training with George, he called me over to the gym counter one evening. "Hey, Tony, I've got a big weight lifting competition next month. I'm going to add a bodybuilding show. It's the Mr. St. Louis and I want to enter you. Let me see you do a double bicep pose."

Man, if he thought I was ready for competition, I was going to give him the best double bicep shot he'd ever seen. I went through eight different poses I'd learned from the muscle magazines. There was dead silence. By now all the members at the gym had gathered around to watch. George looked at me and said loudly, "Hell, my two-year-old grandson can pose better than that. I think you're hopeless. Now I've got to teach this fucking kid how to pose, too?"

Coming out from behind the counter, he stood next to me and began hitting a couple of his best poses. When he finished he leaned over to me and whispered in my ear one of his most famous one-liners, "I still fucking got it!"

As I continued to practice my eight poses, he went back inside his office and got on the intercom to reprimand one of the members. "Hey, screwball! Yeah, you in the gray sweat top. If you bang that weight together one more time I'm going to make you wish you'd never been born when I'm done kicking your ass."

I kind of smiled to myself. I liked George's tough talk. It was nice knowing that he kept an eye on every member and wasn't afraid to speak his mind.

Preparing for competition, circa 1976

With his encouragement - actually, it felt more like an order - I entered my first two bodybuilding competitions, the Mr. St. Louis and Mr. Missouri. I was built up with excitement and anticipation, along with confidence, thanks to George. I trained and posed intensely trying to perfect my technique. I had no other thoughts on my mind other than gearing up for my first title at the age of 19, the youngest contestant. All I cared about was being crowned Mr. St. Louis, then Mr. Missouri. My picture would be in all the newspapers and muscle magazines. Maybe even Mom, wherever she was, would read about me.

I was brought back to reality when I failed to win either of the contests. I placed third in the Mr. St. Louis contest and sixth in Mr. Missouri. It was a huge disappointment not winning the titles. I could hardly accept it. What was I doing wrong? I surely didn't blame George. He had done everything he could to transform me from a skinny kid into a well-built bodybuilder. Mr. Camp expressed his condolences, as did members of the gym, while I bet some were feeling I was a little too big for my britches as it was pretty obvious I was one of George's favorites by the special training he was giving me.

The next day I walked around with my head down, depressed and still trying to figure out why I wasn't the champion. Later in my career, I'd learned to keep my expectations low and hope for the best. But at the time, as a kid back then, I had convinced myself I was going to win. George saw how down I was and offered a little pep talk.

"Tony, you got a third a couple of weeks ago and a decent sixth the other night. There were some tough fucking guys up there who've been training a lot longer than you. We'll continue to train hard and come back next year and kick their asses. Pick your head up, kid."

"Okay, thanks, George," I said, but I didn't feel any better.

The thought of coming back next year to the same contests was more than a downer. To me, that wasn't progress. I was so upset. To make myself feel better I went and picked up the latest issue of *Muscle Builder and Power*, one of Joe Weider's magazines, from the rack of bodybuilding publications that George kept at the gym, and immersed myself in reading about Arnold Schwarzenegger and a few other pros. They were pictured working out at Muscle Beach, in Venice, California. The sun was shining, people were strolling along the boardwalk, and everyone seemed to be in good spirits.

There and then, my dream of going to California without a doubt became my mission. It became my obsession and I couldn't wait to move out West. At that moment I felt something come over me that was pushing me to do it. "Man!" I said to myself. I'm going out there and join those guys. I'd become a pro bodybuilder.

Plans began to materialize in my mind. There was nothing to keep me in St. Louis. I had already planned on leaving home as soon as I graduated from high school. As previously mentioned, after many years of poor school attendance and failing grades, I'd been put back a year so my age at graduation was 19. I decided to skip the ceremony. Any walking across a stage in the future would be to collect a bodybuilding trophy, not some piece of paper.

Now that I had the specific goal, I needed to start getting an actual plan in motion. But there was one big moment I was dreading.

CHAPTER 21

I walked into George's office. I was very hesitant about telling him I'd come to a life-changing decision.

"What's happening, kid?" He said, looking up from some papers on his desk.

"Um…er…George…um…"

"Spit it out, Tony. What is it? I don't have all damn day."

"Well, um," I swallowed nervously and blurted out, "I want to let you know I'm moving to California. I want to become a professional bodybuilder. That's where all the best bodybuilders train."

Forgetting that he had the intercom turned on, George immediately went into one of his famous rages. He stands up and slams his fist on the desk. With his loud voice he began to shout. At this point the whole gym had stopped their workouts to witness first hand the fiasco that was about to unfold. I hadn't expected this crazed reaction.

"Are you fucking kidding me?" He screamed. "You can't be serious. You're never going to make it. You placed 3rd at the Mr. St. Louis and 6th in the Mr. Missouri. What the hell do you think your chances are to win anything out there? There are 15-year-old kids with bigger arms than yours. California is the mecca of bodybuilding. That's where Arnold trains, for God's sake. Where did you get this foolish idea, anyway? Answer me! Don't just fucking stand there all wide-eyed!"

His words cut through me like a knife. Where was the guy's assurance to me that I could be a champion? What happened to his belief I had the potential and talent to compete with the best? I'd lived on that faith for all the months I'd trained with him and now all of a sudden he was taking it all back.

"Um...I've been dreaming about going to California for a long time," I stuttered.

"That's the problem. You need to wake the fuck up because it is only a fucking dream. You've really lit my fire today. Hell, I need to calm down. My lunch is ready. Get next door and pick it up."

I did as he ordered, picked up his lunch, and came back into his office. Placing the food his desk, I leaned over and whispered, "George, you forgot to turn the intercom system off."

"FUCK!" He reached over and switched it off. "Take a load off, grab that chair, and sit down," he said.

His anger appeared to have been spent, but he still had a straight face. I figured he'd thought over what I'd told him while I was next door at the restaurant, and he'd come to a decision. I was right.

"Well, kid, if you're going to move out there, go down to Gold's Gym in Venice and look up Ken Waller."

I knew Waller had trained at George Turner's gym but didn't realize he'd gone out to California.

"Tell him I sent you," George continued, "maybe he can help. I'm not good at giving speeches, but for your information, this can be a cruel, fucking world, especially out there in California. You're so damn naïve. You've got to be careful. That place, if you let it, will destroy you. With that being said, if you don't fuck up with getting caught doing some stupid crime, you'll make it."

I was excited to hear his favorable words. Here was the George I knew, the trainer who had faith in me. The other remarks, the negative ones, I took with a grain of salt. Perhaps I'd surprised him with something he didn't see coming.

He continued, "I've installed enough grit in you that I'm sure you'll be able to fight your way through whatever they throw at you. If you ever fucking need me, give me a buzz."

That was quite an offer and I was extremely grateful. George Turner had trained some of the best bodybuilders around and now he was putting his reputation on the line for a kid like me. We shook hands and I went home. With his blessing I could truly enjoy the excitement I had felt ever since making my decision. I was ecstatic! I couldn't wait to share my new plan with my sister Carolyn.

By now I had found out the cheapest way to get to California, and where the Greyhound bus terminal was located. I had very little money in my pocket. Enough for the bus ticket, but it didn't enter my mind to be worried about it. There was no way on this planet I wasn't going to go to Los Angeles.

I thought of asking Scott to come, too, but I guessed Madir would never agree to it. Instead, I approached Shawn Wade, another one of my good high school friends. An African-American, he was outgoing and a superb all-around athlete. He was a year younger than me, 18, and a great guy.

We were playing basketball in the school playground and shooting a game of 21 when I brought up the subject of leaving town.

"Hey, man," I said dribbling the ball, shooting a skyhook, and winning three points. "You know I've been talking about going to California?"

"Yeah," he said, shooting the same shot. "We're even."

We continued playing as we talked, with Shawn claiming he would win 21-3. "Well, I think we should both go to California," I said. "It's the place, bro. All you've got out there are beautiful beaches, palm trees, and a lot of hot chicks everywhere. It's like going to paradise."

"What're we going to do out there? How are we going to live?" He asked.

"Don't worry about that. We'll figure it out when we get there. Nothing is happening here. What do we have to lose? We can always come back. I just know that's where we've got to go, man." I was full of assurance. I still had no idea why I had no doubts that it was the right thing to do. George Turner believed in me and I just knew instinctively that my future lay out West.

Shawn didn't give me an answer that evening as we joked back and forth over our scores, and finally he won, again. The next day I reminded him about going to California. He said, sure, he'd come with me. He seemed serious about it and I was enthused. Everything was falling into place.

It was time to tell Carolyn. I went over to her best friend's house where she was living. As I came down the sidewalk she was standing outside, looking at her watch.

"Hey, sis. What's going on? What have you been up to?"

We hugged. "Working my butt off!" She said. "Thank God I've got the next two days off. So, little brother, what gives with this pleasant surprise? You never come around much."

I was quiet for a moment, trying to find the right words, a gentle way to let her know I was going to the West Coast. I'd be cutting all my ties to everyone I knew in St. Louis and Memphis. I had no idea if and when I'd ever be back. Well, that was looking too far ahead. And yet, something told me I'd be leaving for good. "I've wanted to see you because I have something real important to tell you."

"Please don't tell me you've got some girl pregnant. You'd better not, boy!"

"No, Carolyn, it's nothing like that." I looked away from

her for a moment, then looked back at her. "What I want to tell you is, um, I've been thinking a lot, and, I've decided to move to California."

She looked stunned for a moment and I wondered if she believed me. "You're kidding, right?"

"No, my friend and I are leaving next week."

"What friend?" She asked.

"My friend Shawn from school." I guess I looked and spoke seriously enough for her to realize what I was telling her. She began to cry.

"You can't. Please don't leave me here by myself. We've got nobody else, it's just us, you and me. You can't leave! Tony, please don't go!"

Man, I hadn't imagined that this would be so hard. My sister was right, we only had each other. The rest of our family was scattered who knows where. But the lure for California was too much to resist. I had to get out there. I didn't know how to comfort Carolyn except to hug her close. She pulled away, took a tissue from her purse and wiped her tears.

"I'm sorry," I said. "I love you, sis, but it's something I've got to do. I must go."

"This is crazy. Please don't do this." She begged. "When are you coming back?"

That was probably one of the most difficult questions I've ever had to answer. I hadn't really thought that far ahead. Yet, I somehow knew what I had to say. "I'm not coming back."

Carolyn's painful expression showed her disbelief. "How long have you been planning this? You've never said a word about leaving."

She sure knew how to make a guy feel guilty. "It's been a while now." I stood there in front of her, kind of shuffling my feet and feeling a little ashamed that I hadn't confided in her earlier. Yet, my plan had only truly come together when Shawn said he'd go with me.

"You don't have any money," Carolyn said. "Who do you know out there? No one! It's too far from home. We won't be able to help you if you need it. Suppose you don't make it?"

"I've never thought about not making it." I answered. "If I don't, then it's in God's hands. But I'm not going to change my mind. It's all I think about. For some strange reason, I feel that I just have to do it. That's it."

My sister began sobbing. Then she said, "oh my God. Well, all right. You know I'm going to miss you. Please be careful. Take care of yourself. I love you."

I was on the verge of bawling, too. Being adopted by Madir, and finding my sister, and all of the friends I'd made had been very special to me. Now, I was about to leave them all behind.

"I love you, too," I said.

Another hug and we parted. While I felt sad at leaving the one and only sibling I had contact with, nothing could diminish my excitement at the bold step I was about to take.

CHAPTER 22

The day to leave St. Louis arrived. I had barely slept all night. I packed my stuff into my little beat-up dark brown suitcase with two pairs of jeans, a couple of T-shirts, a pair of shoes, and some sweats. Everything else, I wore. In the pocket of my black, hooded jacket was every dollar I had to my name, $75, most of it earned from returning my graduation outfit Madir had bought me, and doing odd jobs.

The Greyhound bus terminal on South 15th Street was a single-story building near the St. Louis Blues' arena. Shawn and I were boarding the bus when I saw Carolyn come running towards us. We stopped and stood in the open doorway. I had a big smile on my face.

Carolyn, 21 years old

"Sis, what a surprise! What are you doing here? How did you find us?"

"I wanted to see you before you leave. How did I find you? You know me, boy, I can find you anywhere, little brother. It's my job to look after you." She replied.

When I introduced her to Shawn she wanted to know how old he was. He told her, eighteen. "You boys," she said. "I'm so worried about you guys going out there without knowing anybody. Shawn, what did your parents say about you going so far from home?"

Shawn shrugged. "They think I'm crazy, but I'm old enough to make my own decisions."

"I know you boys are old enough to make your own decisions, but aren't you aware how extremely dangerous this is? This is real life. It isn't a movie. It's not a game. I was hoping I could come down here and change your minds. But, I can see you are both determined to do this. How much money you boys got?"

"My mom gave me a hundred dollars," said Shawn.

"I've got $75," I told her.

"Well," Carolyn was speechless. "Uh, I don't know what to say. I guess there's nothing that I can say other than I'll be praying that you boys will survive out there. Tony, please call me as soon as you get to Los Angeles."

"I will, I promise."

Carolyn, teary-eyed, said, "give me a hug!"

I did, then we went back into the bus to our seats. As we pulled away, Shawn and I both waved to her. I could see she was still fighting back tears as she waved back.

We knew the trip was going to be arduous. Five days on the bus, but at least we were able to choose where we sat, thanks to the 1964 Civil Rights Act. We spent most of the time eating all our junk food, and of course we had some healthy meals too that Madir made. Shawn's Mom packed food, as well, that we shared.

We looked out the window excitedly as the bus left via I-44 and I-40 West, taking us out of Missouri and right on through Oklahoma, and Texas, the state I thought we'd never get out of. I can remember stopping in Amarillo and other cities that I was familiar with because I'd seen them on a map in school. Eventually, we made it out of Texas and the bus headed through New Mexico, Arizona, and then, California.

As soon as we saw sand in the desert we were overly exuberant. We were almost in paradise. We honestly believed that Hollywood was the place of easy living.

We pulled into the Greyhound bus terminal on 7th Street on a hot and muggy summer afternoon in downtown Los Angeles. Everyone piled out of the bus, stiff and hungry from the long journey. Outside the terminal, it was a different world from the Midwest. Smog hung in the air; trucks, cars, vans and buses hurried by; freeways packed with vehicles buzzing past; people filled the streets rushing every which way. It felt like I had arrived on a different planet, one far removed from the slow pace of St. Louis, and it was overwhelming. Walking along the sidewalk, mouth agape, staring up in awe at the skyscrapers I accidentally wandered into the street, narrowly avoiding a collision with oncoming traffic. "Hey, nigger!" the driver yelled. I'd never heard that back in St. Louis.

Shawn and I, he with two suitcases, me with just one, walked slowly down the street, looking around. We were both traumatized and confused. This wasn't exactly how I'd pictured California. Where were the beaches, the hot chicks?

"This is crazy," I said to Shawn. "It feels like I've just landed on Mars. I've never seen so many people of different races."

"Yeah, I know. It's kind of scary. We're so far from home." Shawn replied.

"I'm trying not to think about it." I told him. "Man, it's so crowded, dirty and noisy. Nothing like St. Louis. Hey, there's a hotel about three blocks up. See the sign on the wall? Let's head that way."

"After five days on the bus," said Shawn, "a shower and some real food is a must right now. Otherwise, I'm going to lose it."

"Hold on, we're almost there." I said.

We reached the Hotel Cecil, a two-star, eight-story hotel, and went inside to register. The atmosphere in the lobby back then felt like a flophouse. It wasn't far from Skid Row, and I learned later that the hotel was mostly for transients in those days. Our room cost $7 a night. It faced the street and was as loud inside as if we were out on the sidewalk.

Ten days later, Shawn and I had been eating one meal a day at a nearby buffet cafeteria with our money running out. Shawn totally lost it and he didn't pull any punches letting me know how he felt.

"We've been sitting here without a plan of how to get out of this jungle. It must be amateur hour," he said angrily. "L.A. sucks! We never made it to the beach. Dude, we're two days away from being homeless. I can't take it anymore. We really didn't think it through and we don't know anybody out here."

Frustrated, I said sadly, "I know." Shawn had the television turned up trying to drown out the noise from outside. I was sitting on my bed, with my head in my hands, staring at the floor. I knew Shawn was right. We were broke and had no idea what we were going to do next. I looked up at him.

"Calm down, man. We'll figure something out."

"No, dude, I'm not going to calm down!" he shouted. "I'm eating one meal a day. I'm starving. I don't have any money left. I'm leaving! Come on, man, let's go back to St. Louis."

That was the last thing I wanted to do. I didn't care what it might take but there was no way I was going back there with my tail between my legs. I was committed. At the same time, I was worried sick about our predicament.

"I can't," I said. I was dejected, too, but nowhere near enough to give up and return to St. Louis. "There's nothing for me to go back to. Don't leave. How am I going to make it on my own?"

"It was your whole idea to come out in the first place," he yelled. "You figure it out. I'm out of here."

I told him, "That's fine! You go ahead and go. I'm staying. This is it for me."

Shawn sat on his bed and picked up the phone on the nightstand. He called home. "Hi, Mom."

I could hear her reply. "Hi, baby. How are you? We're missing you, Shawn."

"I miss you too, Mom. Hey, I'm in a bad way. The situation out here has gotten really messed up. I'm out of money. I need a ticket home. It's like living in the freaking jungle. This place is horrifying. We're trapped in downtown L.A. We never made it to the beach." His words ran into each other, he spoke so fast.

"Calm down, baby. It's going to be all right. I'll go down to Western Union first thing in the morning and take care of it."

"Oh my God, thanks, Mom. I can't wait to get home." When Shawn hung up the phone and turned towards me his face was alight with happiness until he saw the expression on my face.

"Aw, man, I'm sorry. Why you don't ask Carolyn to send you some money for a ticket home? No, I guess not. You are determined to stay here and make it work. Well, it could man, but I don't see how."

The day after Shawn left to return to St. Louis, I unexpectedly collapsed out of terrifying fear of being alone and trapped in downtown Los Angeles. Carolyn was right, no one was coming to save me.

CHAPTER 23

I couldn't breathe, my chest hurt, and I felt like I was having a heart attack. I managed to stagger to the hotel front desk to ask where the nearest hospital was.

Luckily, it wasn't too far away. I thought I could walk there if I took it slowly. Hanging onto the side of building walls as much as possible along the way. After a short time, I reached the Emergency Room.

A nurse took me to an empty hospital room and asked about my symptoms. I was still clasping my chest. "I feel like I'm having a heart attack. I'm sweating and shaking. I can't catch my breath. I feel like I'm going to die."

"Have you ever experienced this before?" Asked the nurse.

"No, ma'am."

"Do you have any other health issues?"

"No ma'am."

"Please lay down. We need to check your vital signs."

The nurse gave me a brown paper bag, told me to breathe slowly into it, and told me to stay in the bed until I was breathing normally. She checked my pulse, blood pressure, and temperature, and said everything appeared to be normal. "There's nothing physically wrong with you. You're in excellent health. Have there been any stressful events occurring lately?" She asked.

Man, if she only knew! I revealed to her. "Yes, ma'am, there have. My decision to come to Los Angeles with my friend from St. Louis has been extremely stressful. It's scary out here now that he's left. I don't know where to go and I'm almost broke."

"That explains it, then. I'm sorry to hear about your difficulty, sir. You were hyperventilating and having an anxiety attack. That can happen when you're overly stressed. Try to stay calm. I'm sure things are going to work out for you."

I appreciated her sympathy and thanked her, but it sure didn't solve my problems. I had $9 left in my pocket. Where should I go? How am I going to eat? This was probably the lowest point in my life at that stage. I was 19 years old and in good health, except for the stress, but I had no way to earn a dime.

I checked out of the Hotel Cecil and walked to the nearest bus stop. I decided to take the very next bus that came along and ride it to its last stop, wherever it went.

The next bus to arrive at the bus stop traveled to points west. I had no idea what that meant but I got on with my little suitcase and sat down. The surroundings and scenery began to change for the better the farther we went and I began to hope I'd made the right decision. Once we were out of ugly, dirty downtown, we passed nice apartment buildings, and homes with yards. The traffic didn't ease up that much but now it was mostly cars and vans. Passengers got off at various stops. Pretty soon I was the only person left.

The bus driver pulled up, and turned around to me.

"Santa Monica Boulevard and Rodeo Drive. This is the last stop," he said. Wow! I knew those names. Santa Monica was where Muscle Beach was, and Rodeo Drive was an upscale shopping district. Man, did I ever land on my feet! I was excited, relieved, and exhausted all at the same time.

In a kind of daze I got off the bus with my suitcase and looked around. The sun was shining, and sun-tanned girls in flip-flops and shorts and guys in T-shirts with beards and ponytails passed me by. Everyone looked relaxed and pleasant. I had no idea which direction to head in. As I stood on the curb trying to figure it out I looked up and saw actor Richard Burton casually crossing the street. Of course! I was in the heart of Beverly Hills. He was dressed all in white. The whole scene seemed surreal to me. I needed to sit down a moment and take a deep breath.

A few feet away was a bench with an African-American young man sitting there alone, reading a muscle-car magazine, it felt as if he was somehow waiting on my arrival. He had the biggest, most awesome Afro hairstyle I'd ever seen. It had a pick sticking out of it. As I approached he nodded and when I joined him on the bench he held up his hand to shake.

"Hey man. You work out?" He asked. He sounded really friendly.

"Yes," I said.

"Where're you from?"

"St. Louis. I've only been out here for a couple of weeks." I replied.

"Man, you need to go to Muscle Beach. That's where all of the guys work out, my brother. You need to go take the bus to Santa Monica Boulevard and Second Street."

"Yeah, that's where I'm supposed to be heading, for sure."

I asked him for directions and which bus to take. We both got up and he walked me a little ways, then pointed to a different bus stop. He flashed me the peace sign and went back to the bench where he resumed reading his magazine.

I waited a while and not too long after came the bus. I got on, sat down and set my suitcase at my feet. I asked the driver to let me know when we got to Second Street in Santa Monica. Santa Monica Boulevard seemed endless, it just went on and on.

I looked enthusiastically out the windows, and finally I saw the Pacific Ocean ahead! It was sparkling in the sun and seemed to be so peaceful.

The driver didn't need to tell me when we were at Second Street. I knew we'd arrived because the boulevard dead-ended at the beach. I picked up my suitcase and walked to the front of the bus, waiting for the driver to stop and open the doors. I stepped out onto Second Street and breathed in the warm sea air. I couldn't believe my luck in getting on the very bus in downtown Los Angeles that would take me directly to the beginning of the fulfillment of my dream.

Instead of going over to Muscle Beach right away, I decided to go to Gold's Gym and seek out Ken Waller, the professional bodybuilder George Turner had advised me to meet. Set a block back from the beach, Gold's had a storefront with two huge windows displaying posters of bodybuilders and contest winners. It was an old building in a string of shops that had been spruced up. Joe Gold was a former pro bodybuilder himself and had designed and built unconventional gym equipment specifically for bodybuilders. When I went there for the first time, Joe didn't own the gym any longer. He'd sold it to Ken Sprague in 1972. The name remained the same as it was famous all over the world.

I pushed open the door and entered. My eyes immediately going to the great champions I recognized from the muscle magazines I'd been reading for years.

Among them were Frank Zane, Franco Columbu, Dave Draper, and others, all working out. I was in awe when I saw the amount of weight they lifted doing squats, bench presses, pull downs and other exercises. The athletes were fully focused. The atmosphere was one of extremely high energy, no one talked, and all I heard were weights clinking together. The space was small and the equipment was crowded together, mostly free weights and cable machines. I remembered reading somewhere – or maybe George told me – that bodybuilding was a progressive resistance exercise to control and develop your musculature. Innovative words, maybe, but a perfect description. And these guys were doing just that.

I wasn't sure what to do amid the pros intense training pace, so I went and sat on the floor in the corner, near the back exit. Joe Weider was there, too, with his photographer taking pictures of Frank Zane. Ben and his brother Joe were from Montreal, Canada, where they founded the International Federation of Body Building, IFBB, in 1946. They published several magazines and would later create the Mr. and Ms. Olympia contest. They moved their organization to Los Angeles in the early sixties. Typically, when you win the Mr. America title you are automatically put under contract with the Weiders. They controlled the IFBB and, in accordance with the rules set by the Federation, the athletes were required to abide by them.

After a while, during which I simply took in the incredible scene, unable to believe I was actually watching my idols go through their routines, a well-built guy in his 40s called to me from behind the counter. He was obviously a bodybuilder, and the manager.

"Hey, kid, what are you doing sitting over there in the corner? Get over here."

He had a Midwest accent and seemed a little intense. I walked over with my face, I am sure, reflecting my excitement and wonderment while at the same time feeling kind of anxious.

"Yes, sir," I said. "I see Mr. Weider over there and the photographer taking photos of Frank Zane. I've seen all these guys on TV and in the magazines. Wow! That's Bill. Manny. Danny, they're all here. I've never seen anything like it. I made it! I'm at Gold's Gym!"

I was probably babbling like a kid when I looked over in the far back corner and saw Ken Waller. He was brutally training his legs performing squats. "That's Ken Waller, right?" I said to the manager.

"Yup."

"Well, sir, my trainer told me to ask Mr. Waller if he could help me, oh my God, he's huge! I'm afraid to go over there. He seems very serious."

As I spoke, Ken set his weights back on the rack and went through a door marked Locker Room. It didn't occur to me that, in any case, I should never interrupt someone when they were working out. I'd forgotten that rule in my elation of this amazing moment of witnessing some of the best bodybuilders in the world.

"Your trainer, you said?" The manager was looking at me with a skeptical expression on his face. "I can't imagine you having a trainer."

I didn't blame him for that remark. While I'd built up some bulk, it was nowhere near any of these guys. "Yes, sir. George Turner was my trainer. Hey, is Arnold here?"

"No, he was in a couple of hours ago. Where the hell are you from, kid?" The manager's tone had turned kind of chilly.

"St. Louis, sir. I've been in L.A. for two weeks."

"Do you want to buy a membership?"

"I can't afford it. I don't have any money. Can I please work out for the day?"

"No. If you can't buy a membership, I'm going to have to ask you to leave," he said, frowning. "We can't have you hanging around the gym."

He came from behind the counter and opened the front

door. I picked up my suitcase and left, embarrassed and chastened. It hadn't turned out the way I'd envisioned meeting with Ken Waller and asking him for help. I'd tried, and failed. Yet, mixed in with my misery was a feeling of anticipation that it would all work out. Where that notion came from, I have no idea. Maybe my faith and remaining hopeful. I knew I needed to believe in myself enough to keep going forward, toward my goal.

Thrown out of Gold's Gym, but understanding the manager's action, I decided to go to Muscle Beach like I'd originally planned. I asked a guy for directions who was standing outside the gym how to get there. He told me to go a block over to the beach, make a left, and the Weight Pen was just a few more yards down.

I walked over and there I was, standing on the famous Venice boardwalk. I headed south like the guy said. I was completely taken by surprise with the incredible sights of the ocean and the beautiful palm trees, the array of entertaining acts dressed in all sort of colorful outfits as the large crowds of people lined the boardwalk, standing watching them perform some unbelievable stunts. There were girls in bikinis, jugglers, roller skaters and panhandlers. You name it, it was here, just like I'd seen on television in back St, Louis. I said to myself, *this is paradise*. I'd never seen anything like this until now. What I did know was this is where I wanted to live.

I arrived at the Weight Pen. The place was epic, filled with guys hard at work lifting some very heavy weights during their punishing workouts. The Weight Pen itself was built of concrete with a green weather-resistant type of carpeting covering it. It was surrounded by a fence and had a gated entrance. I knew without a doubt this is where I needed to be. I overheard a guy a few feet away from me telling his friend how, a few weeks earlier, he'd seen Arnold Schwarzenegger training down here with his friend Franco Columbu and how they were joking around and seemed to amuse themselves between sets with all the locals and even with some of the massive crowds of tourists. He went on to say how funny it was to see the tourists for the most part standing in awe of the two great champions.

Wow! Oh, my God! I'd only hoped to have seen Arnold down here! On every national holiday there was a bodybuilding competition on the stage for local bodybuilders who were starting out with hopes of moving up to bigger and tougher shows throughout the state of California.

It cost $3 for the week to work out at the Weight Pen. I went to the Weight Pen's office and the guy running the office never charged me the fee. I guess he could see I was very poor and maybe felt sorry for me.

"Forget it, kid," he said warmly.

"Thank you, sir," I replied. I asked if I could leave my suitcase in the office. "Sure," he said. I placed it on the floor next to his desk and went into the Weight Pen.

I was so excited to be working out as it had been a while since I'd trained. It was before I left St. Louis. Hard to believe I was now training in the Weight Pen where a lot of top pros came to work out. There were posters on the bulletin board of bodybuilders like Arnold and another guy named Kalman Szkalak who was making a side chest pose. His chest was enormous and completely shredded, I mean, what a crazy shot! It's etched in my mind forever. I found out later he was the current AAU, Amateur Athletic Union, Mr. America.

After my training and watching the scene until the sun went down and the bodybuilders had left, a full moon came up. I wondered where I could sleep. I had eight dollars to my name and needed it to buy some cheap tuna fish and Gatorade, whatever I could find to help me survive.

I hitchhiked up to Santa Monica, which I thought was a safe part of town, and I came across a church. I seemed to be drawn to it. I was so scared when I went behind the church and laid down on the ground in a fetal position. I pulled up the hood of my jacket to cover my head and then I rested my head on my little old beat-up suitcase, terrified, but eventually I fell asleep.

When I awoke the next morning a priest was peering down at me. His kindly face was a welcome sight. He told me he could take me to the church's homeless mission, where I could get a free meal. I followed him and got my first breakfast in days. Afterwards, I went into the sanctuary. A service was in progress and I sat down in one of the rows of chairs, still trailing my suitcase.

The priest gave the homeless people there an encouraging, uplifting message. At one point he went around the sanctuary inquiring of each of us about our circumstances.

"I want everyone to feel welcome," he said. "This evening, at the end of the service, we'll be serving dinner. So now, I'll make my inquiries starting with the young man sitting in the middle row. How did you end up in this difficulty, and what are your hopes for the future?"

With a slight quiver in my voice I answered right away, "I'm from St. Louis. I came to L.A. through faith and a dream. I'm looking for a change, a better life. My hope is to get a job and get on my feet."

"You're a very brave young man," the priest said. "God has plans for you. Continue to walk in faith. God loves you. God bless."

"Thank you, Father, sir."

I left my suitcase at the church, got directions and made my way to the local unemployment office. Looked like my luck was about to change for the better.

CHAPTER 24

The unemployment office was packed with people sitting on chairs and standing against the wall. Kids were running around, and it was very noisy. I was given a number, 74, and told to wait to be called. After an hour I heard 74 announced and went over to sit in front of the lady who'd held up a card with my number on it. Telling her I would take anything available, she had an opening for a maintenance job about 18 blocks away. She asked if I had a car. "No, ma'am."

She told me to head east on Colorado Blvd. When I got outside the unemployment office, I saw a young man about my age who had been in line with me. He got into a car, and I thought nothing of it. I began walking and counting off the blocks. I finally arrived at my destination, with my old black sneakers still holding up, and went into the business office of what I believed was a factory. I didn't care what kind of work they did here, I desperately needed the job.

"How can I help you?" Asked the receptionist at the front desk. I showed her the pink slip from the unemployment office. "Oh, I am so sorry," she said, "but that position has just been filled by the other young man from the unemployment office."

At this point I completely broke down and began sobbing uncontrollably. My disappointment and stress were so intense I started to tremble. All my hopes rested on getting this job. To find out it had gone to the other guy because he had a car to drive here and had arrived first was devastating. I was once again in total despair. Things couldn't get any worse, because I knew the instant I walked out of that door my life would be over.

"I'm sorry, ma'am," I could hardly speak, "but I walked eighteen blocks to get here. I haven't eaten for the past two days except for a meal at a mission. I don't have any money, only fifty cents in my pocket. I don't know what I'm going to do." I said, as I stood there sobbing my eyes out.

The owner of the business must have heard because he came out of his office and told me to wait a moment. He went back into his office and returned shortly. "This is for you, young man," he said, handing me a check for fifty dollars. "May God bless you."

I thanked him tearfully. To this day I believe that fifty dollars was a defining moment in my life, one of many that ensured my survival. The money was a Godsend and perhaps another sign not to give up and to keep following my dream. I don't remember how I cashed that incredible fifty dollar check. All I knew was that I had two twenties and a ten in my pocket and I felt a tremendous surge of relief. Life wasn't hopeless, after all. Again, I had scraped through to another day. I slowly walked the 18 blocks back to the beach.

CHAPTER 25

T he next day I worked out at the Weight Pen extremely harder. Ever since I'd arrived, I'd been spending as much time as possible at the Weight Pen. I had no job and had plenty of time on my hands. I spoke to hardly anyone, I kept mostly to myself.

Just as I finished my workout a few days later, a Caucasian gentleman, who I guess was in his early forties, approached me about taking some nude photos. He explained they'd be very artistic and tastefully done. Being nineteen years old I was really offended and insulted by the offer. Where I'm from, back East, St. Louis, this was unheard of, especially in 1976. Nude photos of any kind of men and women were strictly a taboo subject. The only chance of seeing nudes were in *Playgirl* and *Playboy* magazines. I'd personally never known anyone who had this sort of material. I thought to myself, *This is a whole other world out here, definitely free spirits*.

About the offer, I thought, why not, do it, you could for sure use the money. I was pretty convinced that no one that I knew would ever see them. Being so young and naive, I believed that the only people who secretly purchase this type of magazines and photos were abnormal.

Over the next few years we'd occasionally shoot at different locations around Los Angeles. Like way up in the mountains and at expensive homes around town that had spacious

108

gardens with statues in their back yards. Never did we shoot at the beaches, though. There wasn't a lot of money involved as a way of payment but in my dire situation, a little money became very helpful.

I'd decided not to spend the money on a room. I bought a little food, as I was eating the bare minimum. Something I'd become accustomed to growing up.

1976

Periodically, I'd wash the few clothes that I had, T-shirts and shorts at the restroom sink on the Santa Monica pier late at night. Then walk the brief distance to the church to sleep.

A couple of weeks or so later I was hanging out, of course, at my favorite place at the Weight Pen when a pleasant-looking Caucasian man approached me. He was probably in his fifties, wore glasses, and looked physically fit. I'd see him and a lady that I assumed was his wife working out at the Weight Pen off and on. "Hi," he said. "I'm Jason Warren. What's your name?"

"Tony, it's nice to meet you, sir."

"I don't mean to disturb you," he said, "My wife, Susan, and I have seen you here before. We are school teachers and we were athletes back in college, and even these days, with our busy schedules, we're still dedicated to staying in shape. It's not easy, but we're doing our best." He had a nice smile, and over-all seemed like a decent person. He continued, "We just love the outdoors, and train here when we can, mostly on weekends. We heard you're alone and have been sleeping behind a church in Santa Monica."

"Yes, sir, I've been looking for a job, but I've had no success so far." Then he said.

"My wife and I couldn't imagine someone in your situation. You seem like a good kid who's down on his luck. If you don't mind, we would like to offer you a place to stay. It would be temporary, of course, until you got on your feet. We're both teachers at Santa Monica City College. Our two kids are grown and they are also teachers at a local elementary school in Los Angeles."

A place to stay? Man, was this for real?

He went on saying, "We believe if you can help someone in need then that's what you should do. We've always taught our kids to do the same. So now, we have this huge house all to our-selves, just around the corner from the college. There's an extra room you can have, if you want it."

Did I ever! Oh my God, this is amazing! I thought to myself. Just when my circumstances couldn't get any more desolate. I felt as if it was me versus the world my entire life and that has been a heavy burden to carry. The workouts helped, but I still couldn't see any light at the end of the tunnel. I didn't have a real trainer anymore, although some of the bodybuilders at the Weight Pen would give me a bit of advice and show me a few exercises. But basically, I was on my own. Feeling lost, I'd found myself searching, trying to figure out who I was. "Yes, Jason, sir, I'd be very grateful for your help. Thank you!"

Just then Susan Warren came over, and Jason introduced her to me. We shook hands. "Tony, I think you're going to like where we live, it's in a secluded neighborhood." she said.

"That sounds great, ma'am."

"So, shall we go?" Jason asked.

"Yes, sir!"

After I moved my meager belongings into the Warren's house and checked out my spacious bedroom and bathroom, I decided to apply for welfare as the unemployment office had so far turned out to be a dead end. Again, the government assist-ance office was crowded and chaotic. Little kids were screaming and crying and their mothers looked exhausted trying to cope with them. I went to the machine that spat out numbers, and then stood near the door where there was a space between two guys and I waited.

When I finally heard my number called I went to the partitioned counter where a welfare officer was seated. "How can I help you?" Asked the lady.

"I'm sorry, ma'am, but I'm in a real tough place right now. I need to apply for some assistance, please."

"You shouldn't be embarrassed, young man," she said kindly.

"When I was growing up my Auntie Bettie taught me never to ask for anything. You had to work for everything you got in this life."

"I'm sure your Auntie meant well. Don't worry. It's going to be okay. Our purpose is to assist others in need. Please have a seat." She replied.

I sat down and she proceeded to give me instructions. "First, you have to fill out these forms. Have you ever had assistance before?"

"No, ma'am!"

She could see I was humiliated by the question. "Sorry," she said, "but it's normal policy for us to ask these kinds of questions."

I filled out the forms and handed them back to her. After looking them over she said, "You're Tony Pearson, I see here that you are nineteen years old. Unemployed. Without any family support. Is that correct?"

"Yes, ma'am." I answered, as I felt a deep sadness washing over me.

"Are you looking for work?"

"Yes, ma'am, but I haven't found anything yet. I registered with the unemployment office but they had nothing for me. They sent me on one job interview a few weeks ago but it didn't pan out, and there have been no other leads so far."

"In order to maintain assistance you must continue look-ing for work. We'll need you to show proof here at this office every two weeks that you've been applying for jobs. Is that understood?"

"Yes, ma'am."

"Okay, everything looks to be in order, but I have to in-form you that we can only give you a limited amount of help. After I finish the paperwork you can pick up your food stamps here as early as Monday."

That was only three days away, I said to myself. I thanked her and left.

Consequently, I wasn't on welfare for long. I found a night security job in a Santa Monica nightclub near the college that I could walk to. It didn't pay much, but it was more than the government assistance I was getting. It gave me a good feeling that I was making some progress and left some daytime hours for workouts. I'd sleep most of the morning after coming off my shift and then go to the Weight Pen all afternoon and into the evening if I didn't have to be at work.

By now I'd come up with a pretty good routine for train-ing myself. One afternoon I was performing a set of standing barbell curls targeting my biceps. I could feel the high level of energy all around me as the bodybuilders went through their intense drills. I had just placed the weights down from complet-ing my super set of triceps pushdowns when a biracial young Caucasian and African-American guy came over to me.

"Hey, my name's Robert. I see you're very serious about your workouts. I am, too. I was wondering if you'd like to work out together?"

"I'm Tony. Sure, I'm down. That's a great idea. I'm doing biceps and triceps today. C'mon, jump in."

We fist-pumped and smiled at each other. It'd be cool to have a workout partner after being on my own for the three months I'd been in L.A., I suggested we train everyday around this same time, noon.

"I train six days a week," I told him, "hitting each muscle group twice a week."

"Okay," said Robert.

"Let's start now. You're up, it's your set."

He did a set of standing barbell curls, I took another turn, and pretty soon we finished our workout. We got along really well, and while I was delighted that Robert had invited me to be his buddy, I wondered what surprise fate had up its sleeve for me next. It didn't take long to find out.

CHAPTER 26

After I worked out with Robert I went home to the Warren's and was relaxing on one of their recliners in the back yard when Jason came out of the house.

"Tony," he said, "I've got some good news. Guess what? I've found you an apartment. Today just by chance I ran into an old friend of mine, he's a realtor in the area. He said he came across a little place in Venice, just off the boardwalk. It's a furnished one-room studio. As a favor to me, he's willing to give you the first month free."

Man, it sounded perfect, but with my issues, could I afford it? I loved living with the Warren's but it wasn't the same as having my own apartment.

"How much is the rent, Jason?"

"It's only a hundred and fifty bucks a month. I'm sure you'll be able to afford it, since you've got your little security job now. Here, I've got a couple of Polaroids of it." He handed me the pictures to take a look at. "It's not a big place but it's a start." He said.

A start? I studied the pictures some more. To me it was a palace. "This is awesome, man. Compared to where I was raised. This is heaven!"

"Oh, and to top it all off, since Gold's Gym is about five blocks down the street, you won't need a car or have to take the bus any more from our place. So congratulations, buddy, it's like a blessing. It's been less than a month since you came to stay with us, and now, you've got your own place. You have the chance to have independence and become your own person. This is an essential part of life for everyone."

Jason was always so wise and giving me good advice, and today was no exception. I was extremely grateful and told him so. I was more excited than I'd been in such a long time.

"I've never had a place of my own before," I said, with a huge smile on my face, staring at the pictures. "When can I move in?"

"In a couple of days." Jason replied, delighted with my elated reaction. "I just have to confirm it with my friend."

I couldn't wait to make the move. When I finally got the key, walked into the studio with Jason, and looked around, I was beside myself with happiness to know this place was all mine. I put my suitcase on the floor, checked out the bed, the tiny kitchen with a sink and hotplate in an alcove, and the real small bathroom. I looked out the window that faced onto the street. Across the way was a bus terminal. *How perfect*, I thought.

Jason had brought me a housewarming gift, a cactus plant which he set in the middle of the small coffee table. After he left I put away my clothes and shoes in the tiny closet. I sat down on one of the two chairs in the place and began a more careful study of my new home. The walls were painted a light beige, and on the floor was gray shag carpeting. I opened the cabinet in the kitchen and saw some mugs and plates, a couple of bowls, and a saucepan and a skillet. In a drawer were a few knives, forks, and spoons. The previous tenant had even left some napkins. I realized I didn't need to buy anything to start living like a normal person. The Warren's had been so kind to me, and I intended to stay in touch with them.

On the studio's bare walls I pinned up pictures of famous bodybuilders I'd found in muscle magazines. They were all of my idols. I had a couple of pictures of my sister, Carolyn, to display too but didn't have any other family member pictures. When I arrived in Los Angeles I had made up my mind to leave the past behind me and start a new life.

Robert and I continued to train together. We'd been steadily increasing the intensity of our workouts and the amount of weights we lifted. One Saturday, around 1 p.m., we began our legs routine while listening to Queen, the Rolling Stones, and Jimi Hendrix's "Purple Haze" blasting out in the background on one of the guy's boom box. It was the middle of the summer and the heat was in excess of 100 degrees. There were maybe a dozen of us at the Weight Pen and no one seemed to care about the temperature, not even the crowd that grew denser as the day wore on.

"Hey, man," I said to Robert when he arrived, "don't forget we're doing ten sets of ten of squats. Let's warm up with the 45s. Are you ready?"

"I'm always ready. Let's make this happen. You start."

I did my set and then racked the bar. Robert went over and picked it up, putting the weight onto his back. He completed his warm-up set. From this point on the fight really heats up. Fast forward as Robert is now fighting to conclude his eighth set.

He completed seven reps and stopped "C'mon, Robert, finish it. That's right...eight." I stepped in closer to spot him as it appeared he was in great pain. "That's nine... ten." He barely got through it and racked the weight. Then I took my turn again. The heat was having an adverse effect on our energy level by now but that didn't matter. On the next set I figured I could now raise the stakes a little higher in our continual battle to challenge each other. Robert attacked his next set irrefutably securing his first ten reps.

"Now, c'mon. It's easy." I yelled. "Forget about the numbers. You got your first ten reps, now give me five more."

After barely managing to complete the set Robert replaced the bar on the rack. I added another two plates; we were now up to 405lbs., I picked it up and walked it back from the rack. Robert began to push me. "You can do this man, let's go!"

"No problem," I said. "It's time to step it up. The first twelve I'll make sure not to pause."

I started my set but after the ninth rep I felt a tremendous pain in my quads and began to falter. Robert continued pushing, "You've got to fight, Tony. Give me six more. C'mon, get into it! Great! Fourteen... fifteen. Done!"

By now most of the crowd had moved over to watch us, realizing that the battle had gotten to an insane level. Robert began his next set, squatting like a machine, down, up, digging in deep. The crowd was cheering us on, counting out the reps loudly in unison.

After he finished his set and racked the bar, he dropped to one knee. He was gasping for breath and put his hands to his head. "It's too hot out here, man," he said. "I feel like I'm going to throw up." The crowd murmured in sympathy and some moved away.

"We don't have time for that, man." I replied. "You've got to swallow it!"

He fought to maintain his composure. I knew how he felt because I felt the same way. We both were completely exhausted. I couldn't help but lean against the fence to hold myself up. I didn't want to quit. "It's the last round," I said loudly. "I won't be denied! Not today!" I took the weight off the rack.

A guy in the crowd yelled out, "You can do it, Tony!"

I began the set of squats as if my life depended on it. Through sheer determination I got through it, but after the final rep and just barely racking the bar, I dropped to my knees in complete agony.

Robert looked very relieved we were finished, and we congratulated each other on a great but incredibly tough workout. Talking amongst ourselves, after we had somewhat recovered from the workout, our backs to the entrance, the crowd became suddenly quiet, their faces reflecting awe and disbelief, everyone frozen in place.

I heard a voice and recognized the accent immediately. I turned around and there was the world champion bodybuilder, the best bodybuilder on the planet, standing in front of me. Arnold Schwarzenegger, The Austrian Oak. His eyes were focused on me and it was evident he was going to say something.

Robert took in the scene, grabbed his gym bag and weight lifting belt, and, saying he had to leave because he couldn't be late for work and he'd catch-up with me tomorrow, and left. With the crowd fascinated with the sight of this famous 6ft. 2in. giant of a man, there was a hush as Arnold smiled at me.

Arnold revealed that he had been watching me for a few months and that I trained very hard. I stood there wide-eyed and speechless. He also told me that he though I had a lot of potential!

This was incredibly astonishing to a 19-year old kid. He wasn't that much older than me, maybe in his late twenties at the time, but his reputation and fame were unmatchable.

He'd said in a magazine article that his goal had been to become the greatest bodybuilder in the world, and he sure had achieved that. He was the youngest Mr. Olympia at age 23, and would go on to win the title a phenomenal seven times.

The same year I had arrived in California, 1976, Arnold announced his retirement from competition, but he had so many interests in the bodybuilding industry, writing training books and columns, endorsing products, and owning gyms, he was still the biggest name. He continued to work out at Gold's Gym and Muscle Beach, luckily for me.

He expressed that I was going to be a great champion on that auspicious day. He followed up his prediction with an unbelievable offer. To take me through a workout.

Stunned, I managed to mumble a 'thank you' as he began to demonstrate some chest and triceps exercises. I watched in complete amazement that this legend was actually taking the time to help me train.

He kept showing me exercises as the crowd watched. Finally, when he'd completed with the session, he recommended that I go and see Joe Weider. And to tell him that he had sent me, and he should write an article on me for the magazine. He finished by saying his office was located in Woodland Hills.

Finding a small notepad and pen in his gym bag, he wrote down the address and directions to the Weider office and handed it to me.

I was still in something of a daze and couldn't believe what had just happened. I was more inspired than ever. I knew that being discovered by Arnold was huge. I had talked about achieving my goal, but I hadn't established a real clear plan. But after my meeting with him, I instantly changed my mental approach toward my training and the start of my bodybuilding career. His comments assured me that this was also another marker on the path to my dream. To my astonishment and gratitude, Arnold also featured me a few years later in the first edition of his book, *The Encyclopedia of Modern Bodybuilding*. The entry reads, "I remember a few years ago seeing a skinny black kid training at the Weight Pen in Venice Beach. I watched him doing endless sets of squats, with very heavy weight, torturing himself with rep after rep. After a while, his thighs began to grow and soon they were huge, separated and beautifully defined, and only a year and a half later he entered the Mr. America contest."

CHAPTER 27

B y now I knew that traveling anywhere by bus in Los Angeles took a lot of time, so I left for Joe Weider's office in Woodland Hills early the next day. Before I went home the night before, I'd asked at Gold's Gym which bus I needed to take. As a result, I had to transfer three times before arriving at my destination.

The Weider office has been called the Grand Central of the bodybuilding and fitness movement. Every major industry figure has visited there, some for photo shoots, others to pitch stories, and many, like myself, hoping to be interviewed for an article.

At the reception desk I asked to speak with Mr. Weider. I was offered a seat and the receptionist phoned through into his office. I felt like a kid at Christmas, I was so hyped-up with excitement at meeting this famous man whose publications were read all over the world. I took a seat, and after about thirty minutes Mr. Weider came over to me, looking me up and down, frowning.

He asked how can I help me. I told him my name and that Arnold had sent me. I took three buses from Venice Beach to get here, sir. He wants you to write an article on me for the magazine. Mr. Weider asked if I was sure and stated that it couldn't true, as his frown deepened. I had no idea what he meant by that remark, but then he turned and yelled down the corridor, ensuring one of his writes to write an article on me. Mentioning, I'd said Arnold had sent me.

I sensed that Mr. Weider was annoyed as I stood in front of him bright-eyed, smiling, showing off my shiny front gold tooth and with barely any muscles to speak of. I couldn't have weighed more than 170 lbs., even though I was very muscular. He probably thought to himself, this kid has no potential, and why would Arnold send him out here to interrupt me. Maybe, I should have called first and made an appointment, or he was just having a bad day. He knew Arnold had sent me and very likely he wrote the article solely to please him.

Whatever the case, it seemed Mr. Weider had taken an immediate dislike toward me. Despite my future successes, our relationship was always strained and awkward although I would appear on the covers and featured in several articles in some of his magazine publications in the not too distant future. I was forever devastated that this wasn't what I'd hoped my meeting would turn out to be.

Mr. Weider abruptly walked away and a guy who introduced himself as Jack Neary, who took me back into his office and started to write the article. To my disappointment, for some unforeseen reason the article would sit for two years before it was published. Jack and I spoke for about an hour and half at length before I left to take the three buses back to Venice.

The following day the weather was perfect in L.A. Robert and I worked out and then went to our regular place at the boardwalk café. We watched the street performers entertaining the large energetic crowds of locals and tourists.

"How did it go at the Weider's office?" Robert asked.

"It was unbelievable! I met Mr. Weider himself; he seemed a little bit bothered by me. Maybe I should've called first. But, anyway, they wrote the article on me for their *Muscle Builders* magazine. Man, I'm so excited! This must be a dream. Oh my God! I can't wait until it comes out and everybody back home can see me. They're not going to believe it. When I was back in St. Louis, I used to watch the bodybuilding shows on ABC's *Wide World of Sports* when Arnold won Mr. Olympia. Plus, I've read all of the articles on the pros training routines. This is such a high! I'm really motivated to compete again."

"Great." Robert said. "You know, man, the Mr. Venice competition is in a couple of weeks. You should enter."

"That's a great idea! Do you think I have enough time to get ready?"

Robert laughed. "Get ready? Look at you, man. You're always ready."

"Okay. Starting next week I'll go to the college and run around the track a few laps to help me lean out. You know, I competed in two contests back in St. Louis, the Mr. Missouri and the Mr. St. Louis."

"How did you do?" He asked.

I grimaced at the memory that was still fresh in my mind. "In the Mr. Missouri contest I placed sixth," I told him, "and in the Mr. St. Louis, third. I wonder what it feels like to actually win."

The Mr. Venice competition dawned a clear and sunny September day. When I got to the Weight Pen the weather was perfect. I oiled up with baby oil, believing that my chances of coming in maybe the top three were pretty good. For the past couple of weeks I'd stepped up my training, pushing myself to the limit and practicing posing.

I looked around at the huge, enthusiastic crowd that had already gathered around the stage set-up on the Weight Pen platform for the contest. A really attractive young lady caught my eye as I scanned the on-lookers, wondering if the Warren's were out there. As it was a weekend, many members of Gold's Gym were either competing or cheering us on.

The pre-judging began, and the crowd began noisily applauding their favorites as we took to the stage and went through our routines. The Judges scored competitors on symmetry, muscularity, conditioning, and presentation. Some of the contestants had been members of Gold's for years, others came in from other areas, and most were seasoned entrants. Sure, I had the two competitions behind me, but my total experience was far less than just about all of my rivals. Plus, I was the youngest competitor.

After I had completed my individual posing routine, which I thought went pretty well (I hoped I hadn't made any mistakes). Soon afterwards all of the other contestants had finished their performances. The emcee announced the end of the pre-judging and that the judges would take a few minutes before the final round. He urged the crowd to stick around.

Robert was standing in front of the stage. I went over to him. "Hey, man, how do you think I'm doing?"

He didn't hesitate to say, "Man, you've got this. You've got it! You're in crazy shape today."

"Thanks. Hey, did you see that girl with the dimples checking me out? She was standing over on the left of the stage?"

"Yeah, of course I saw her, she's very cute but I think you should be focused on the contest right now."

He was right. I went backstage and started pumping-up for the finals. For a few moments I hoped the girl would hang around after the contest so I could introduce myself to her, but I pushed the idea aside. Right then all I could think about was the judges' decisions, and how I'd handle the disappointment if I didn't place.

The head judge was sitting at a table along with the six

other judges. They were fighting the heat by drinking water, and all of them wore baseball caps to block the sun. The huge crowd of spectators continued cheering with a variety of top forty music that played in the back ground during the show.

The head judge spoke into the microphone. "May we have all the competitors on stage, please? Thank you, gentlemen. Please spread out and give yourselves room. Some music, please." As the music began, the judge commanded, "Pose down!"

We all began aggressively hitting our best poses trying to outdo each other. We were pushing and bumping into each other as we raised our arms in some of the classic poses. The audience erupted, lively shouting out individual names of the contestants, urging them on. It was kind of a wild scene, being typical of Venice rather than the much more formal bodybuilding contests I'd seen on television.

The emcee got into it, too, firing up the audience and shouting, "Give it up, ladies and gentlemen! Come on. Let them hear you! All of these guys are putting on a fantastic show today."

The audience responded very loudly. It was great to hear their enthusiasm. I sneaked a look at the girl and she was staring right at me, smiling and clapping. Man, I felt great and knew I had to meet her. Even if I lost today, I felt like a winner already with the nice reaction I received from her. I hadn't had time for dating for the longest time, and I'd been concentrating instead on my training. Besides, I've had no money to take anyone out on a date. But now that I had my own place and a little money in my pocket from my job, things could change.

After a few minutes the head judge thanked us and the crowd then announced that the judges had made their final decision. Everyone fell silent with anticipation waiting for the results. All of the competitors were standing on stage in the line-up in a semi-relaxed pose. The head judge gave his score sheet to the emcee who was standing at the podium, announcing. He took his time as he paused to view the scores. "Ladies and gentlemen, "the winner of the 1976 Mr. Venice Beach is...Tony Pearson!"

A rush of joy came over me like never before. I was so excited and amazed that I hardly heard the crowd shouting their congratulations. The trophy girl came over and handed me a trophy. I really had won! I lifted it into the air as far as my arm would reach, smiling broadly, and thanked the judges, the crowd and the emcee. My first win!

Winning Mr. Venice Beach, 1976

CHAPTER 28

I rushed backstage and got dressed as the other contestants were starting to leave, I jumped off the stage and joined Robert. He was smiling, enthusiastically gave me a high five, a big hug and slapped me on the back.

"I told you, you had it," he said as the exuberant crowd surged around us.

"Thanks, bro, for pushing me through all those brutal workouts."

"Don't mention it. It's cool," he replied.

I looked at the trophy. "Wow! Mr. Venice Beach!" I said. "I'll predict I'm going to win Mr. America in two years."

The reason I said that was because my certainty was at an all-time high after winning the show.

Robert laughed. "Calm down, not so fast. You're starting to sound like the real champ, Muhammad Ali. This is your first win, man. It's a tall order to fill to become the best bodybuilder in the country in two years."

"Dude, I'm serious," I said. "I am going to win the title or die trying. I'm willing to do whatever it takes. Pain and suffering mean nothing to me compared to what I've gone through. Winning Mr. America is my only chance to survive. No one's going to save me. I've got to save myself."

No one knew the circumstances of my childhood. I kept all those secrets to myself, buried deep inside of my soul. I leaned in closer to Robert to say, "Plus, when Arnold, the best bodybuilder in the world, believes I can do it, who can possibly say I can't?"

Robert didn't need to reply. He knew I was serious by my intense facial expression. I went to look for the girl with the dimples and saw her standing on the boardwalk. Still holding my trophy I found enough courage to approach her. When Robert saw I was going to introduce myself, he gave me a discreet thumbs-up sign and left.

"Hi," I said. "What's your name?"

"Mia. I know your name. You just won the show. Congratulations!"

"Thank you, Mia. That's a pretty name. What's your last name?"

"Thanks. It's Madison."

"Mia Madison, Wow! That sounds like a movie star's name. What a cute smile you've got."

"You're kind of cute yourself."

We stood there kind of admiring each other. I asked if she was from around here.

"No, I live in West L.A., born and raised." She said. "And you?"

"I live a few blocks just off the boardwalk. You come down here much?"

"Not really," said Mia. "But it's a holiday and I decided that I needed to be near the water. I love the ocean."

"So do I, it's so relaxing." I told her, trying not to look her up and down. "You're in great shape. Do you work out?"

She smiled, thanked me and said, "I work out but not with weights. I like to run. It's the best way to relieve stress. I ran track in High School. I would like to learn the proper way to weight train, though. Working out is so important to me because I feel there should be a balance of your mind, body, and spirit. I guess you could say I'm kind of spiritual."

It was nice hearing her insight. Here was someone who seemed to believe, as I did, about being in balance, and that fate guided our destiny. I knew that people in California tended to be more spiritually-minded than others in other parts of the country, and here there were many people who practiced meditation, Zen, and other kinds of beliefs that were not traditional religions.

"Two kindred spirits," I said to her. "So, are you dating someone?" Before she could answer a passerby yelled out, "Congratulations, man!"

"Thank you," I yelled back, raising the trophy in salute. I turned to Mia again. "Sorry about that."

"No problem. No, I'm not dating anyone at the moment? Do you have a girlfriend?"

"No, I'm single. Hey, my friend is having a house party. Would you like to hang out?"

"Sure." She said, smiling.

I was thrilled. I took her hand and we strolled slowly toward John's house.

I'd met John, a part-time school teacher and bodybuilder, at Muscle Beach. He was in his 30s, a real nice guy. While I was explaining to her who John was, a guy was walking toward us holding a boom box to his ear. The Isley Brothers were singing "Summer Breeze." *It couldn't be more appropriate*, I thought, *being with Mia.*

"How old are you?" I asked her.

"I'm Eighteen. How old are you?"

"Nineteen." I said.

"You're not from Los Angeles. Where are you from?" She asked, with a curious facial expression.

I asked her how she knew I wasn't a local. She said she could tell I was different, in a good way, but she didn't explain any further. I made a mental note to ask her later on what she meant, but right then I was just content to tell her a little bit about myself as I walked with her at my side, holding hands. I said that I was from Memphis, and moved to St. Louis when I was thirteen.

"Southern boy, I knew it," she said. Then she asked, "So why did you decide to move here?"

I told her about my dream to come to California, and to live in Hollywood, that I'd been here four months, and it was the best decision I had ever made.

We arrived at John's house on the boardwalk. The music was blaring with a mixture of soul and dance songs. The place was packed, and people were drinking, smoking pot and indulging in all sorts of things. It was a fun, relaxed atmosphere. Everyone was laughing and joking around. I spotted John across the room and took Mia over to introduce her.

"Hi John, what's up?"

"Tony! Hey, man, congrats on your win. Is that the trophy?"

I'd forgotten I still had it in my hand. "Yeah, thanks, bro. This is Mia."

After she and John shook hands I took her to sit on the sofa. A young kid came over with a soft drink in his hand.

"Tony, right? I'm Terry Lockett."

I'd seen him at the Weight Pen. He was only 17, yet we could all see he had great potential as a champion bodybuilder. He continued, "John sure knows how to throw a hell of a party. I don't want to disturb you, you two make a cute couple."

"Thank you," I said, happily.

"I've been checking you and your training partner out and it looks like you're destroying your legs. You guys are like two gladiators. I mean you don't even talk during the workout. And congratulations on your win, bro. Can I take a look at the trophy?"

I handed it to him and he turned it around to see both sides. He kept on speaking. "I need to get with you, man. I need to bring up my quads. I want to win this show next year."

"Sure, we can do legs," I said. "We're doing legs tomorrow at noon. From what I can tell, you've got potential, man."

He was so excited at my comment.

"Cool man! Right on. I'll be there for sure." Terry thanked me, gave the peace sign, and went over to the bar. I apologized to Mia for the interruption, but she said I had handled it well. I was in one of the most content moments of my life at this party, having happy friends around, and getting to know such a beautiful young lady. Here I was, winning the show and winning the girl! We continued listening to a romantic love ballot. I felt a little poetic, and said, "Music just soothes the soul. What's life without it?" Mia smiled in agreement and snuggled closer. "You said you live in West L.A?"

"Yeah, I live with my mom." She replied.

"Where's your dad?" I asked.

"He's not in my life much, I mean, I know him but we're not close. I'm not a daddy's little girl or anything. It's just my mom and me."

I asked her if she had a job and she told me no, that she'd just started classes at Santa Monica City College where my friends, the Warren's, were teachers. I was pleased Mia went there because it meant she was in the vicinity, probably every day, as the college was just several blocks north on Pico Boulevard.

"What's your plan for the future?" She asked.

Man, did I ever have a plan! It encompassed the entire universe! I was full of eagerness and I was dying to tell her all about it.

"I want to become a professional bodybuilder. I know that sounds crazy. You've heard of Arnold Schwarzenegger, right? I met him a couple of weeks ago down at the Weight Pen. Ever since then I've become obsessed with working out. I can't think of anything else. I mean, I am determined to train hard because I want to be the best bodybuilder in the country."

Mia seemed surprised and fascinated at my intensity and leaned in closer to shut out some of the noise of the party.

"To me," I said, "bodybuilding is like art, you're sculpting yourself. When I initially saw a bodybuilding contest on television, that was my first thought, that the guys looked like walking masterpieces, especially when they were posing."

She nodded, and said, "That's so cool. I admire your focus. You seem to know exactly what you want out of life. I've always believed you should follow your dreams. My ultimate dream is to become an R&B singer like Natalie Cole or Teena Marie. It's a passion of the mind. I can feel the music vibrating through my body and how I'm able to express my emotions through the lyrics. You can tell a story of heartbreak, love, and happiness."

"You're deep. You have to pursue it. I can hear you have a singer's voice. It's a little raspy with a deep tone to it that makes it unique. Hey, there's too much drinking and pot smoking going on here. You want to go to my place?"

She answered by standing up, smiling, and pulling me towards the front door. We reached my little studio in about ten minutes and I led her inside. At the entrance she stopped, and looked around.

"Cute place," said Mia.

"Thanks."

"Are those your motivational pictures?" She asked, pointing at the magazine covers on the walls.

"Yes, they're my idols. Have a seat, relax. You want to listen to some R&B?"

There wasn't any comfortable place to sit, the kitchen chairs were old wooden ones. My single bed pushed up against the wall served as my sofa, and we sat on that while listening to some smooth jams on my tape player that she liked. After a while I put on a romantic love song.

"Oh my God, Average White Band," she said, joyfully. "'A Love of Your Own' is one of my favorite songs. It just came out a few weeks ago."

"I know, A.W.B., they're so cool! I have never met anyone like you. You're really sweet. It's your smile that got my attention."

I offered her the only drink I had, bottled water, and we each had one. Then I kissed her and asked her to dance. We slow-danced for several minutes, just enjoying holding each other. But something was making me nervous, this would be my first time! I kissed her again and we lay back on the bed passionately making out. I gently undressed her and we affectionately embraced in sweet love. It was beautiful, sensuous, and even a little spiritual. I didn't need to worry.

The next morning Mia jumped out of bed, anxious not to be late for school. Before she left, she asked if I'd like to hang out later.

"Yeah, that's a plan," I answered. "Give me a kiss." She kissed me and said, "Mm, those lips."

CHAPTER 29

By now, in early 1977, six months after my arrival in Los Angeles, Gold's Gym had moved to a new location in Santa Monica. It was still close by, just north of Venice. A new manager, Kent Kuehn, was hired and was very kind and helpful that allowed me to train there without paying a membership. He was twenty years my senior. We became good friends, and I was really happy later that year when he had won the Masters Mr. USA and Mr. Universe contests.

I knew nothing about life except for my painful upbringing. Kent sort of kept me in check and advised me on life's tough decisions. I was thankful for his help. Life continued with my regular job as a security guard, even though the pay wasn't much, just a little more than minimum wage. Periodic-

Visiting Kent Kuehn, early 1990s

ally, I landed work as an extra in the movies. I even had a starring role on a television show, *The Man from Atlantis*, staring Patrick Duffy as one of the spa minions. That was exciting, but I was still struggling financially. Forcing me to take on a second part-time job working security with a group of other body-builders from the gym (some of them who were pros). Being the youngest of the group I was grateful to them as they'd helped me secure the jobs.

We worked mostly special events and concerts, events like, the People's Choice Awards and the GRAMMYs. We frequently worked at The Forum Arena in Inglewood, the Embassy Auditorium in downtown LA, and the Santa Monica Civic Auditorium, where Dave Johns had just recently won the 1977 Mr. America competition. Most of the concerts were held at the Forum Arena, where we rubbed shoulders with the likes of Fleetwood Mac and Stevie Nicks, Chaka Khan, Rod Stewart, Kiss, Natalie Cole, Aretha Franklin and many more. Working security there was always events occurring. At a Stevie Wonder concert I was positioned on the floor just in front of the stage for the night. While Stevie was playing one of his famous hits from the album *Songs in the Key of Life*, "Love's In Need of Love Today." Every time he would hit a key on the piano my ears would hurt because I was standing next to the massive speakers and with a full house of twenty thousand fans cheering and screaming. All of a sudden something happened to my abdomen; without even trying my stomach disappeared up underneath in my ribcage. I knew I was training and dieting for a show, but out of shock I reached down and grabbed my stomach, trying to figure out what had happened. Then I realized this was my first vacuum pose. Ever since that night I've incorporated it into my posing routines.

Mia and I were happy together and things were going well. She was still taking classes at Santa Monica College. In the meantime, I was competing in every amateur show that I could in the state of California.

After last year's little success in winning the 1976 Mr. Venice Beach, Gold's Gym Classic, Teen division, it gave me a great feeling. Inspiring me to want to compete even more.

During the summer I'd decided to take a huge leap by making my first National debut competing in the AAU Jr. Mr.

USA, which was held in Lincoln, Nebraska. With the help of a few friends ensuring my travel expenses, I was on my way. It would be my first time flying, and, of course, I was nervous about being thirty thousand feet in the air. After surviving the flight without any complications, I'd began intensely focusing on the show. Without a support system, I felt all alone going up against the best amateur athletes in the country. If you think I was nervous about the flight, it was nothing compared to my nerves when I saw the competitors lining up to take the stage. I kept trying to remind myself to stay calm and focus on what I needed to do. I felt good about my training and diet, which, with my fast metabolism, wasn't an issue. I was known for being razor sharp. My posing had improved dramatically. I thought and I felt as prepared as much as I could've been. But little did I know that on the national level the competition was much tougher than I could have ever imagined. It was the big leagues. I got my butt royally kicked, edging out only a third place in the men's short class.

The flight back to Los Angeles was a long, lonely trip. I couldn't have sunk any lower. It really made me start to wonder if I had what it takes to actually become a national champion. It was a harsh lesson to have learned. For a period of time I fell into a deep depression, something I'd been plagued with throughout my life. Compounded with the terrible loss, it was more than I could endure. But I knew I'd better to hurry and pull myself together and begin training harder if I ever wanted any chance of winning a national show.

The following day I returned to the gym with my head down and in a low spirit. In my heart I was set on making it right and I didn't care if I'd dropped dead from over-exerting myself during my workouts. All I'd ever known was hardship and pain thanks to my Auntie Bettie. If she were here I could only wonder what she'd say. "Ya betta git yer ass ta work, dae cain't stop ya, boy!" It was so clear hearing her say those words. It was as if she was standing in front of me and for certain she'd have given me a backhand, knocking me across the room for good measure, just for showing a glimpse of emotions, which in her world was strictly forbidden.

Training at Gold's Gym was incredible. I mean, imagine working out next to some of the best champions in the world. This was the first time I saw Robby Robinson in person. It was an awesome moment for me. I'd been following his career, and he was featured in all the muscle magazines. He and his training partners were there every day, like me, sometimes twice a day. They were training at an insanely brutal pace.

I was too shy to approach him but I'd taken notes of all their exercises, how they mixed them up, the number of sets and reps, but mostly how they were performing each exercise. I made sure I included them into my workout with my own training partner, Robert. In those days you had to really prove yourself to the pros that you have what it takes to be a champion if you wanted to be accepted.

A few weeks later, still feeling disheartened, it just so happened I was training alone. My training partner couldn't make it. I knew my workout were definitely not at a hundred percent that day. I had too much going on in my head and couldn't find the motivation. I heard a baritone voice behind me say, "You better get your ass to work and stop messing around, T.P."

I turned around and it was Robby promptly walking away. I guess he'd seen I was down on myself and maybe he saw some potential in me that I couldn't see. Perhaps, he wanted to give me a wake-up call. And did he ever! That fired me up from that day forward. It was an all-out attack during my training because I knew he was watching me.

Soon thereafter we became friends. I remember him taking me to see Frank Zane guest pose out in Orange County, CA. I was really excited to be hanging out with the champ.

Robby and I sat in the second row. Frank was the last to take the stage as the guest poser. I was wide-eyed, staring at him as he stood there waiting for the music to start. He began to strike all his classic poses perfectly timed to the music. My mouth fell open, I was astonished at how he grew in size from one pose to another. I couldn't believe I was witnessing Mr. Olympia right in front of me.

That's when I began to understand the art of posing and how important it was. This was after getting pummeled at the Jr. Mr. USA and the mini-speech from Robby. I was more focused than ever. My training partner and I continued to raise the intensity level during our workouts, holding nothing back. Within a few months my physique had undergone a dramatic change, making some major muscle gains with the exercises we were now doing correctly.

I knew the new year was fast approaching. It was only a month before the competing season began. I said to myself, *I've got something to prove*. It starts with the Mr. Los Angeles competition, held in late January. It's going to be a long laborious season. With that being said, this was my main purpose in coming to California, to dedicate myself wholeheartedly, striving to achieve my ultimate dream.

The new year arrived rapidly. I made it past the Mr. Los Angeles with a close win. The next show was the Jr. Mr. USA in Sacramento, California.

Robert and I didn't change anything we were doing during the workouts. We remained intent on assuring I maintained my condition for the show, which I managed to scrape through by winning the title with a score of 4-3 against a very tough line-up of competitors.

After the show, I went back to my room to change before going to dinner. I turned on the television while getting dressed and switched the channel to a new show called "Amateur National Bodybuilding Sports Show," the ANBBS. Nick Cole was the announcer. He was sitting at his news desk reading from a teleprompter. The show was covering the state, regional, and national shows. As he finished giving a full report, he suddenly added, "This just in, folks, a flash report. The Jr. Mr. USA was held tonight in Sacramento, California, and a complete unknown beat out twenty-five other competitors to walk away with the title!"

Then flashed upon the big screen just behind him were photos of the six winning finalists as they were posing against each other, and individually hitting some of their best shots. Moments after he'd shown a couple of photos of me with the trophy in my hand, he continued with, "Tony Pearson, someone we've never heard of! We here at ANBBS will be paying close attention to the Mr. California, the next show leading up to the grand finale, the coveted Mr. America contest, which will be held in early September in Cincinnati, Ohio, at the Cincinnati Music Hall. This is Nick Cole wishing you all a good night."

Yes, I won, but just barely. My two shows had been really close calls. I felt good I'd won but, I knew my toughest challenge was in a couple of months against the most shredded bodybuilder in the country, Ron Teufel. It was going to take every ounce of my being to upset him.

Everyone had arrived at the Mr. California competition and got settled in. Starting the following morning it was an exhausting fight all day during the pre-judging. My class was full of competitors because most men are usually medium height. I had to dig deep to find something extra to narrowly win my class by the smallest of margins. I breathed a huge sigh of relief but the real fight was just about to begin.

After the show I went directly back to my room, threw my gym bag into the middle of the floor, went into the bathroom and stared into the mirror. "What happened?" I asked myself. I stormed back into the bedroom and turned on the television. As I flicked through the channels and came across a late night edition of the Nick Cole show. He was on announcing. I went and sat on the edge of the bed to watch. Nick announced that he had a special updated, Flash Report: "This evening, at the Mr. California event, there's been a complete destruction by bodybuilding sensation Ron Teufel. He destroyed the entire field of forty five competitors, including his rival, Tony Pearson, who won his class but was no match for the knockout punch of Teufel. Bets have it that Teufel is a sure favorite to make a clean sweep of all three amateur shows this year by winning the ultimate crown, Mr. America. That has never been done before. After such a crushing defeat, Pearson's chance of winning the title has dropped significantly among insiders and fans alike. This is Nick Cole sounding off. Thank you for tuning in!"

He was right. I was dealt a crushing blow. I wanted to throw something at the television. *Oh my God!* I didn't know how to react. Should I scream, cry, or yell? It was like a knife stabbing me in the heart.

I woke up earlier than usual the next day, resolved to work harder than ever. I didn't allow myself to lose faith. Maybe, this was a good thing that I needed to happen. But I don't think I'd become complacent. I managed to rebound from the devastating loss and went on to win the AAU Jr. Mr. America a few months later. I surely wanted to win the Mr. America title. But serious doubt had crept into my mind about my chances; however, I had to keep it together. My survival depended on it. I knew if I didn't win, I'd for sure end up homeless like when I'd first arrived in Los Angeles. As a result of my work condition had recently changed when I received a notice that the company was downsizing. Whoever won the Mr. America usually went on to financial success, even though it was still an amateur event. All the great bodybuilders had risen in the ranks to join the pros by competing in it first.

When I got to Gold's Gym, as early as it was, there was a huge crowd outside looking through the windows. When I entered, I saw that the place was jam-packed and filled with energy. There was a strong sense of excitement, more than normal. What was happening?

CHAPTER 30

The competitors and even some of the pros were all training. Each one was surrounded by fans and other athletes watching them go through their workouts. Then I saw the cameras. I recognized news and sports reporters from several Los Angeles television channels and others from around the country.

I found my training partner, Robert, already there. I looked around to see if one of the T-bar rowing machines that were mounted on the floor was available. One was free. We walked over to it and began our workout, all the time trying to keep an eye on the media action.

Most prominent was a large TV crew from Cincinnati. Jake Wilson, the sports announcer for Channel 5, was making the rounds interviewing competitors, onlookers, the gym manager Kent, and Gold's Gym owner, Ken Sprague.

"Hello, everyone! This is Jake Wilson coming to you live from the Mecca of Bodybuilding, the famous Gold's Gym here in Santa Monica, California," he said to his television audience. "We've traveled all the way from Cincinnati, Ohio, to get a first-hand look at some of the contestants who will be competing next week for the coveted Mr. America title. Never before in its history has this contest received so much media attention. The build-up to the show has been phenomenal due to the fact that a practically-unknown competitor who has been lurking in the shadows and could possibly pull off the biggest upset of all time."

With that statement, everyone turned toward where we were working out. There was a thunderous applause. I tried to smile assuredly at Wilson where he was standing next to Ken at the front desk because deep inside my tough loss to Ron Teufel was still heavy on my mind. It disturbed me terribly.

Wilson resumed talking. "This young man was discovered two years ago by the iconic six-time Mr. Olympia, Arnold Schwarzenegger. Since then, Tony Pearson has been on fire, winning almost every amateur show in the state of California. With one week to go, Gold's Gym here is packed with fans and reporters from all over the country. Tony and his training partner are in the middle of a vicious back workout. Let's tune in for a quick peek."

He and his crew came over and began filming as I began my set. "He's performing what they call the T-bar row," Jake said as his voice got even louder. "Tony and Robert are showing some fierce intensity and ferocious aggression, folks! Oh, my goodness, it seems they're in the zone, as if they're on another planet. Every rep is precise and on point. I've never witnessed anything like it," he passionately told his television audience. "They're down to the last set," he said. "Let's listen in to hear the battle between them."

Robert was on the machine. "Add on two more plates," I told him. He did, then he finished his set and I replaced him. The camera crew zoomed in. I began rowing with every ounce of strength in my body, feeling my back muscles pumping-up insanely.

"C'mon, Tony," Robert said. "You've got to pull. That's it! Bring it! Two more reps, Eleven... twelve. Good set."

By now everyone had followed Wilson and his crew over. Some of the spectators were standing on benches to get a better view. Robert replaced me on the T-bar and I began to push him forcefully.

"You've got to finish strong," I said. "Give me twelve. Pull harder! Get into it, mind over matter. Okay, that's it, the last two. Eleven… twelve. Nice set! We're done."

We high-fived each other and took off our weight lifting belts, grabbed our gym bags, and headed for the exit. Before we could reach it, Jake rushed over to stop us.

"Excuse me, Mr. Pearson. I'm Jake Wilson from Channel 5 News in Cincinnati. Can we ask you a few questions?"

"Sure, no problem." I said.

"Thank you. First of all, what an intense workout you guys just displayed. They say you're the new rising star in bodybuilding. How do you feel about that?"

"Thanks for the compliment. Rising star, I wouldn't go that far," I replied, half smiling. "I'm here to give everything I've got to be the best that I can be."

"From my understanding you've won a couple of national titles this year, the Jr. Mr. USA and the Jr. Mr. America, is that right?"

"Yes, I did. It's an honor to have won, but that's not my ultimate goal. One week from now is what I've been training for and focusing on for the last two years."

Jake held the microphone closer to me, saying, "Those are some very prestigious titles. It's quite an accomplishment! On the other hand, though, the burning question that everyone has, including the media and fans, concerns your loss to your adversary, Ron Teufel, at the Mr. California a couple of months ago. He received perfect scores from all seven judges. How do you explain that?"

"I salute him," I said. "He's a great champion. He won fair and square. I'm not going to stand here and make excuses. That was my first time challenging him on such a big stage. I mean, the Mr. California is a major show. I misjudged my peak and came in a little off. You take the loss and you use it for motivation."

Jake raised his eyebrows, then said. "You're a huge underdog going into the show. How does that affect your psyche going in?"

"That's the best possible position to be in. It allows you to focus on the task at hand without being overly publicized," I told him.

"How do you feel about your shape?"

"I've made a vast improvement since the California competition. I'm feeling pretty confident. We did everything we needed to do. I feel this is by far my best shape ever."

I struck a couple of poses as the cameraman zoomed in. Jake asked me what my chances were of winning the overall title. I told him I was going out there to do everything possible to win, and that it was then up to the judges. After I stopped posing, he asked if I'd use my posing abilities to my advantage.

"Absolutely," I said. "You have to use every weapon in your arsenal."

"All of the observers and insiders have your rival, Ron Teufel, a favorite by a hundred to one. It seems your chances are very slim. With that being said, I can sense you're a quiet warrior preparing for a serious epic battle." Turning toward the camera, he continued. "Speaking to this young man, ladies and gentlemen, I have a feeling this is going to be the most exciting contest ever! There's definitely something brewing and I can hardly wait to witness this spectacular event." Jake turned towards me. "Thank you, Tony, for taking the time to speak with me, and good luck in the show."

"It's my pleasure. Thank you." I said.

Jake and his camera crew then headed directly over to Ron Teufel on the other side of the gym, near the entrance to the front desk. He had just completed his workout and was wiping the sweat from his face with a towel around his neck. Then he signed a few autographs for some young fans. He was surrounded by his entourage when Jake spiritedly engaged him.

"Mr. Teufel, I'm Jake Wilson from Channel 5 News in Cincinnati. We're going live today throughout the country. Can we get a brief interview with you?"

"Sure you can," Ron said.

Jake first congratulated him on his win at the USA's, and went on to say, "Incredible."

"Thank you," said Teufel.

"You look phenomenal. How are you feeling? Are you ready for next week?"

He answered, seeming very sure of himself. As the cameraman zoomed in for a close-up of his face, Teufel replied, "No doubt, I couldn't be more ready. I feel great. No one is going to beat me."

Jake came back with a question that appeared to have shake up my opponent. "I'm sure you've heard there's been some speculation about your rival, Tony Pearson, that he could be a tough challenge against you to claim the title."

As the cameraman pulled back to get Jake and Teufel from the waist up, Ron's demeanor changed as if on a dime. His answer to Jake let him know what he was really thinking.

"He's not even a thought. After I got a perfect score at the Cal from every judge, it proves that he's no threat. He was lucky to have won his class. He's afraid of me and he should be. This is my year and no one is going to stand in my way."

Jake seemed to be in shock as he tried to collect himself.

"Oh, man," he said. "Those are some very strong words. I can tell you are determined to back them up. You are definitely a man on a mission. It's been a real pleasure speaking with you, and good luck in the show."

144

After they shook hands and Teufel thanked him, Wilson wound up his broadcast by looking straight into the camera, saying, "So there you have it, ladies and gentlemen. Things are really heating up. Stay tuned, as we'll be bringing you the play by play leading up to the biggest competition of the year. Who will be the next Mr. America?"

CHAPTER 31

I arrived at the show in Cincinnati feeling upbeat and ready. I was pretty sure I was in my best shape possible. The hotel lobby was full of excited fans as I made my way to the registration desk and got my room key. I wasn't here on vacation, that's for sure. I went straight to my room and ate a can of tuna, some cooked rice that I'd brought with me for dinner. I'd seen Teufel's routine, he was quite the poser. He always knew how to get the crowd on his side, which only exacerbated the pressure I was feeling. I'd heard he was determined to make history by garnering all three shows within the same year. I was simply fighting to survive in the hope of making a living.

There were other competitors in the show from Gold's Gym. During the middle of the night before the show, we all met in the hotel hallway for a posing session. I'd been practicing my posing daily for the past month. Going up against Teufel and the other competitors wasn't going to be easy. Posing was still fairly new to me, but I knew I had to be flawless and maintain my concentration in every pose in my routine and the pose downs, not to mention being physically conditioned to sustain the energy level that was needed throughout each round of competition. After two long meticulous hours of going through my poses, I told the other guys I'd had enough, fearing I'd burn myself out, and went to bed.

The Music Hall was filled to the rafters with five thousand

enthusiastic fans. There was the judges' table, and the media area packed with reporters and photographers jostling for position in front of the stage. The contestants were all backstage. I said hello to those few I knew. But mostly I kept to myself, as I cleared my mind for battle.

Jake Wilson was at the announcer's table, broadcasting live. He introduced himself to his television audience and welcoming everyone to the 1978 AAU Mr. America competition. His deep voice became louder and more energetic.

"We've finally arrived, ladies and gentlemen, for this massive showdown that has been building up with anticipation for the past two years. All the trash-talking and speculation will soon be put to rest. This is the moment of truth to determine who will be the next Mr. America. This place is buzzing with excitement. I've been told there's standing room only in this beautiful Music Hall!"

At those remarks the audience cheers and applauds became deafening.

"This prestigious show," Jake continued, "started way back in the 1930s, but only in the last few years has it captured an incredible amount of media attention, elevating it to rock star status. Tonight's show is the most watched sporting event of the year, second only to the Super Bowl. Without further ado, let's check in as the competition has already gotten under way. This morning all of the competitors went through rigorous pre-judging rounds to determine who will make it to this evening's final round of class winners. The competitors were split-up into three classes. Short, Medium and Tall."

He paused as the television station's news studio replaced the Music Hall shot to show a petite blonde sitting behind the news desk.

"Good evening," she said in a soft-spoken voice. "This is Marie Johnson. Thank you for joining us for this special sports news edition. Today, our top news story is sports, and what a day it has been. Last year the Mr. America competition was held in Santa Monica, California, along with the Mr. America parade. Tonight, we are so honored to be hosting this very distinguished event. In fact, we are dedicating our entire newscast to the show. We'll be going back frequently to the Music Hall to check in with Jake, who has been there all day. Jake, are you there?"

The picture switched to Jake who was standing backstage. "Marie, yes, I'm here. You don't know what you're missing!"

"I know. I wish I could be there. What's going on?" Jake explained to Marie that he was very surprised that a bodybuilding show had such a high intensity level onstage and among the spectators. "I've never felt anything like it," he told her. "It's a feeling you'd get at a heavyweight boxing match."

"Wow, that's incredible. This is going to be an amazing show," Marie said excitedly. Jake continued to describe the situation. "It's been a very dramatic show all day as well, starting with the pre-judging this morning and leading up to the finals tonight. I've been informed that this is the strongest field of competitors in the last twenty years. Ron Teufel was the obvious favorite. He's the current Mr. California and Mr. USA," Jake said. "However, he ran into a bit of unexpected trouble as he barely pulled through to win his category. Winning by the smallest margin with a score of 4-3. That just goes to show the depth of the competition. The newcomer Tony Pearson won his Medium class fairly easily, and the Tall class went to Manny Perry."

"Ladies and gentlemen," said the emcee, as he tried to speak over the resounding cheering from the audience. "Here we go, these top three finalists did an outstanding job this evening and have won their classes. And now, first to perform his individual routine, our Short class winner! Ron Teufel." The energy in the place was electrifying; the audience cheered at the top of their lungs as Ron delivered a sensational performance. After he'd finished his routine the emcee thanked him for a great show. Teufel energetically raised one hand overhead with a clinched fist acknowledging the crowd, then bowed and left the stage.

Marie and Jake conversed back and forth, with their broadcast being carried live on big screens that were positioned around the venue. I'd been waiting just off stage for Teufel to complete his routine because I knew I would be next. I'd gone through my routine a thousand times in my mind and I'd practiced it endlessly. But for some unexplained reason the Tall class winner, Manny Perry, was called to perform ahead of me. Manny Perry was from Gold's Gym, I knew him quite well. He played as the double for the "Incredible Hulk" television show. He brought the house down with his powerful routine, and the audience loudly applauded and chanted "Manny! Manny!" The emcee gave his thanks to Perry, who completed his performance and made his way backstage.

"Ladies and gentlemen," shouted the emcee, as I continued waiting in the wings. "It's been an amazing evening. Now, may we please have our Medium class winner on stage! Show your support, let's make him feel welcome!"

The audience responded tremendously. I remembered how I never thought to smile. At that moment I was extremely psyched up. I had no other emotion other than focusing on completing my routine without making a mistake. I could vaguely hear the crowd cheering but I wasn't concern about that, all I wanted was to push myself extra hard, flexing during each pose until it hurt to ensure I could possibly have a slight chance of winning. I heard the emcee say "Thank you, Tony Pearson," over and over, but I said to myself "Keep going," I'd determined to complete my performance, because I knew my best poses were at the end of it. The curtains closed in front of me at the one-minute allowed posing mark. As the curtains reopened again I was still posing, that's when I heard the roar of the crowd going crazy, cheering themselves into a frenzy.

I kept posing for another 45 seconds (as I was told later) before completing my routine as I'd broken the one-minute rule. Jake was completely taken back at what I had done. He became greatly animated. "Marie, it's unbelievable what just happened!" He yelled into his microphone. "Each of the final competitors, as you know, are only allowed one minute for their posing routines. At the signal the curtains closed on Tony, but he remained out there, and when the curtains opened again he was still hitting his best poses, over and over, faster and harder! That extra forty-five seconds seemed to have given him the courage and a determination that has infected all of the spectators here. It's an absolutely euphoric moment! If the final pose down is anything like this free posing round, we're in for a colossal history-making showdown!"

Marie said how exciting it was and that everyone in the studio were anxious to hear who'd won. "You won't have to wait much longer, Marie, here come the three finalists!" Jake replied ecstatically.

Teufel, Perry, and I positioned ourselves onstage. I took the center spot between them. For some reason, it just felt right. The crowd was still cheering and applauding insanely loud. The head judge told us to spread out and give ourselves some room. Jake was telling his television audience about the tension that had been building for the last two years.

"There's undoubtedly no love lost between Teufel and Pearson," he said. "The seriousness on their faces tells the whole story. These two young warriors can't wait to get after each other. Pearson is glaring aggressively as he takes up his place, and Teufel looks just as grim."

The head judge called for the music to begin and for the three of us to "pose down!"

As we did, Jake said, "Oh my God, Teufel is wasting no time coming right after Pearson, flexing his abs and showing his calves, seizing upon Tony's lack of calf development that Ron figures will give him the margin for victory. He's pointing to his own calves in comparison to Pearson's, as if asking the crowd, 'How does he expect to win without any calves?' In response, ladies and gentlemen, Pearson remains undaunted and unflappable as he counters by pointing to his quadriceps, as if to reply, 'With these legs, Ron.' Tony is now hitting his extremely shredded thighs, abs, and back poses. He's throwing innumerable muscular poses, taking it right back to Teufel. The audience is overwhelmingly loud, this is exhausting just to watch!"

Jake went silent for a moment as if to catch his breath, then continued broadcasting. "Oh my, they are toe to toe battling it out. It's like two gladiators trying to outdo each other, trying to force their opponent to quit, but neither of them will relent. Pearson came here as a complete underdog, but he's showing the heart of a lion. In my opinion he's the Rocky of Bodybuilding!"

The TV cameras swiveled to the third contestant, Manny Perry, who was posing but stood to one side as if he didn't want to engage in our fierce battle.

"Ladies and gentlemen," said Jake. "This pose down is the longest in history!" He energetically proclaimed.

Ten minutes had passed and the judges didn't tell us to stop. I guess they were enjoying the epic duel as much as the crowd. Ron and I would glare at each other going into a pose fighting with everything we had. Then Jake said, "The judges seem to be having a tough time making a decision. Of all sporting events, this has to be the purest form of competition that I'd ever witnessed." I felt as if I was on the verge of collapse but I knew I had to continue to fight.

The head judge finally told us to take a break as they had made their decision. He handed the score sheet to the emcee to announce the results. There was complete silence among the audience waiting to hear who'd won. You'd feel the immense tension in the air. The emcee took his time as he studied the score sheet and then addressed the audience.

"Ladies and gentlemen, the winner of the 1978 Mr. America title is... Tony Pearson!"

It seemed as if the Music Hall was being shaken off its foundation from the instant explosion of the crowd. There were some boos but the cheers were much louder. Teufel looked stunned! He was utterly surprised, couldn't believe his ears, completely losing his composure with a sudden outburst. He grimaced as if in great pain, clasping his head with both hands screaming, "Rip-off! Fucking rip-off!" as he walked around the stage for a couple of minutes in disbelief. Finally, as I held out my hand to shake his, he slapped it away out of anger as he rushed offstage in total disgust at the decision. Perry and I were in shock. We stood frozen staring into space. For a brief moment out of complete exhaustion, I'd thought the emcee had announced me in third place, but then it hit me, I realized I'd won. Magazine photos later showed the whole incident, with Ron holding out his hand as if pleading with the judges.

Winning Mr. America, 1978

Jake went berserk, screaming into his microphone, "Marie, he did it. It happened! It happened! There's pandemonium throughout the Music Hall!"

Marie, finishing up her news report at the Channel 5 news desk, sounded bewildered in reply. "Jake, what? What happened?"

"This kid from St. Louis, Tony Pearson, has pulled off the biggest upset of the century. Oh, man! Oh, my goodness. He predicted he would win it in two years. He's done it! He's done it!" He sounded breathless as he told Marie the result.

"That's awesome," she said, "Wow! Oh my God, what a show! The excitement here in the studio, too, is tremendous. Thank you, Jake for reporting. What a night! Please tune in tomorrow evening for the six o'clock news. We'll be interviewing Tony Pearson, the new Mr. America winner. You don't want to miss it."

CHAPTER 32

The next evening after the show I went to the Channel 5 television studio for the interview with Marie. As I walked onto the set the camera crew and others standing around applauded, which gave me a comfortable feeling. Marie was charming, and we went on the air live. After welcoming me as the new Mr. America, she thanked me for coming on and asked how it felt to have won the title. "I don't know. It's surreal!" I said. "You get so worked up preparing for the show, and then, when it's over, it takes a few days to calm down and let it all settle in."

"How old are you?" She asked.

"Twenty-one."

"You were such an underdog going into the show," she said, "How did you manage to remain relaxed under so much pressure for all those months?"

"I just tried to stay focused on what I needed to do. I avoided listening to the naysayers who were always in my ear. And kept telling myself anything is possible."

Marie seemed enthralled. "There's an incident that happened during your free posing. You were instructed to finish your one-minute allowed routine, but you defied the command and continued posing for another, from my understanding, forty-five seconds. Is that something you planned to get the judges in your favor?"

"No," I replied in a serious tone. "It wasn't planned. It was an instinctive reaction of survival. For me, this was more than a show. It was a fight for my livelihood." My answer may have sounded overly dramatic to Marie with the shocked facial expression she gave me.

"I must say, the pose down was the most intense ten-minute battle ever, yet you seemed, as Jake said, unflappable through it all. Mentally, what were you thinking?"

I smiled and replied, "You're not thinking, at that point. It's almost like an out-of-body experience. You're reacting to the fight, trying to counter your opponent pose for pose."

"The national media have dubbed you the Rocky of Bodybuilding. What's your reaction to that?"

"It's a huge compliment. I mean, I can clearly see the similarity. Rocky and I are both out there fighting to survive, just in different arenas."

Marie nodded as to agree. "The sport of bodybuilding is still fairly new to the general public. I know it's a lot of hard work and dieting to achieve that level of conditioning. But, my sources have revealed to me that you were living on tuna fish, coffee, and water for the last eight weeks prior to the show. Is there any truth to that?"

"Yes," I admitted. "It's true. I know it sounds a bit extreme but I had to ensure there wasn't an ounce of body fat anywhere. In bodybuilding your diet is the most important part of your preparation for a show. Your goal is to achieve what we call an ultra-shredded look. That's when you can easily identify the details and separation of each muscle group, something like looking at an anatomy chart."

I smiled, enjoying her questions so that I could answer as a way to educate her viewers about our new sport, who might know nothing about it, or us as athletes.

"Also," I told her, "in my circumstances that's all I could afford, tuna and water." I wasn't ashamed to say it.

"That's unimaginable. It must take an incredible amount of discipline and determination. I'm sure a lot of health and nutritional companies are lining up to have such a fine representative. Has anyone reached out to you yet?"

I'd only won the title last night. I wasn't even sure everyone had heard the news yet. I told her, "No," and added, "I was hopeful to receive a few endorsements and exhibitions."

My answer to her next question gave me an opportunity to share my philosophy about my chosen career.

"The popularity of bodybuilding has grown enormously in the last three years. Maybe you can tell us what bodybuilding entails?" Marie curiously asked.

"I don't want to be known as a bodybuilder. I see myself as an artist. There are many different aspects to being a bodybuilder. Of, course, there's the competitive side but I envision the body as a blank canvas. When you work out you're building, shaping, and molding it, creating an aesthetically balanced physique, just like a sculptor who spend years to create a single masterpiece of art."

"That's incredibly fascinating. What's next for you?"

I told her I was going to New York to appear on the *Good Morning, America* show, and in December I'd be making an appearance on the *Merv Griffin Show*.

"It's been a pleasure having you." Marie stretched out her hand. We shook. "I can honestly say for everyone here at Channel 5 we admire your humble disposition, Tony, and we wish you all the best in the future." I thanked her for having me on the show and left.

A week later Ken Sprague and I flew to New York for the television interview on *Good Morning, America*. The female interviewer kindly welcomed us to the show. We took a seat on the sofa. Then she asked, "Tony, can you show us some of the routine that you were judged on to win the competition? We'll take your microphone off." She reached over, removed the microphone from my shirt, and spoke to Ken. "You can explain what we're seeing, Ken, and we'll have Tony take his shirt off, too."

I got up and took off my shirt, and walked to the mark she wanted me to stand at.

Ken began to explain. "You might notice that when he was sitting here beside me, Tony looked like your average college half-back type, but now that he's standing there, of course, he's very muscular. But he doesn't, uh, he's not overly as big as you'd anticipate."

I continued going through my routine. Then Ken humorously laughs, "Now, soon as he flexes of course, it all comes alive."

With Ken Sprague, backstage at the Good Morning America show, 1978

The interviewer wanted to know about the poses I was going through, and Ken explained the various poses. He said, "The idea of posing is to show your muscles, the shape, size, symmetry, and the lack of body fat. That's the whole criteria of judging."

"Why do they oil themselves?" She asked Ken.

"They oil themselves lightly for better light reflection, which is important in any sort of display." I completed my routine and sat next to Ken on the sofa.

"Are people sometimes embarrassed to look at your muscles? Does that embarrass you to have people feel this way?" The interviewer asked me, holding the microphone closer to me.

"No, no," I said. "It feels good." My remark made her laugh slightly, then she brought the interview to an end, thanking Ken and me, and we left. The interviewer's naive line of questioning illustrates the newness of the sport at the time.

Although bodybuilding had just begun to catch on to the general public, of course, leading the way was Arnold Schwarzenegger as he appeared on every muscle magazine cover in the world and had received vast television exposure, national and international, which give the sport creditability. Fans from around the country and around the world regularly visited the famous Gold's Gym in Santa Monica, California, excited to meet some of the professional bodybuilders that they had only seen in the muscle magazines and on television.

I was glad to get back home and settle down to a normal life again even though I wasn't sure what was normal anymore, since I'd won. I did know, though, that I wasn't content to stop at that title. I had greater ambitions.

Mia and I resumed our relationship. "Congratulations, baby," she said in her cute sweet voice. "Mr. America! You're my Mr. America. You looked amazing. I didn't get to see you on *Good Morning, America* because I was on my way to school. How did it go?"

"Really good. You know I'm shy, so Ken did most of the talking. They had me take my shirt off and pose. That was fun."

In a determined voice I said, "Now, I've got my heart set on being the best in the world. I want to win Mr. Universe. It might take me a couple of more years but I don't care how long it takes,

I'm going to do it."

"I know you can do it baby!" Mia said encouragingly.

We started fooling around, kind of wrestling, and listening to the soundtrack by the Stable Singers singing, "I'll Take You There." Mia at once had me pinned down. We were giggling the entire time. She said I was always wanting to play around, like a big kid.

"Maybe I am a big kid, because I never really had a childhood." I said.

"Why not?" She asked.

Still giggling I told her. "It's a long story. I'll tell you about it one day."

Did I really mean that? Did I actually want to dredge up all those terrible memories? My early life was in the past. It was history, and nothing could change it. My new life gave me a chance to live my dream. Sure, I had barely any money, but I had just won the biggest title in the country. My luck was bound to change for the better, I'd hoped. As Mia got the best of me during the wrestling tussle, I told her how much I loved her and she said the same to me as we kissed passionately.

CHAPTER 33

Happily, the following year, 1979, began with a pleasant encounter on a sunny, Sunday afternoon. The boardwalk was bustling with tourists, artists, entertainers, roller-skaters, and the ever-present crowd of people watching the bodybuilders work out at the Weight Pen. The loudspeakers were belting out Donna Summer's latest hit, "Last Dance." I was just leaving the Weight Pen where I'd visited with a few friends when a guy rushed up to me on roller-skates. I could tell he was part of a roller-skating dance group with the way he was dressed. Roller-skating was at the height of its popularity at the time. I would every so often go down and sit on the back wall at Venice Beach to watch them perform on the concrete walk way in the large park area.

"Hey man! Remember me?" He said, grinning happily. "I'm the guy you met in Beverly Hills at the bus stop a couple of years ago. You'd just arrived from St. Louis."

I thought to myself of all the people who live in LA, what are the chances of meeting him again. I stopped in my tracks and looked closer. He was shirtless and wore a pair of black tights and black leg warmers. Still cool as ever with his laid back L.A. swagger and the voice to match. His hair was the same huge Afro with a pick in it that he had when he'd told me which bus to take to Muscle Beach.

"Wow! This is a surprise," I said, smiling. "Yeah, I remember you. What's happening, man?"

"Life is chill, my man," he said.

"It sure is a small world out here," I told him.

He replied in his cool, hip voice. "Right on. L.A. is a hard place to make it, but you did! You made it through my brother!"

"Thanks in part to you for showing me the way, my friend. I'm grateful for your help."

"It's nothing, brother man. What's the word in your world?"

"I'm bodybuilding now. I'm trying to turn pro, very soon."

"Right on with the right on," he said. "Tear it up. You're gonna to be great. Peace out. Stay cool!"

I returned the peace sign he gave me as we wished each other well. Then he skated away.

After three years in California I still appreciated the friendliness and informality of people out here. I loved Venice and Santa Monica, and everything about the place that I'd dreamed about. I felt grateful to be living it.

Just by chance, I had an amazing experience a few weeks later. I was thrilled to meet Muhammad Ali again. At the time, I happened to be friends with the fastest man in the world, Houston McTear, an American sprinter and international track star. He was a member of the Muhammad Ali Sports Club, and he invited me to a party on the Queen Mary ocean liner docked in Long Beach. Muhammad Ali was McTear's sponsor. The party was for Ali's friend, Wilma Rudolph, the champion Olympic sprinter and international track star, as well. It was an elegant affair and everybody was dressed formally. I stood in awe at the entrance to the Grand Ballroom trying to take it all in.

Houston was making the rounds greeting people when I

saw Muhammad Ali come walking down the hallway towards the entrance of the ballroom with his wife, Veronica, and their entourage. I headed towards him, remembering all those years not so long ago and how he played a huge part in shaping my life. When I approached him, he stopped. I was holding a muscle magazine for him to sign. I asked him for his autograph. He wanted to know if I'd won a title.

"Yes sir. Mr. America. I was so honored to be able to tell him of my victory."

He took the magazine and signed it. I thanked him and he and his group made their way to the VIP table where Wilma was already sitting with friends. Seeing him again I felt such gratitude as I recalled that earlier meeting. To me, he was surely the greatest of all time.

An unexpected but exciting and career-changing situation (which I'd greatly resisted at first) presented itself at the front desk of Gold's Gym. Owner Ken Sprague was speaking on the phone. Soon afterwards, he hung up and turned to me.

"Tony, do you have a few minutes?"

"Sure. What's happening?"

"I have an idea for the Mr. Los Angeles contest that's coming up in a couple of weeks. Something that's never been done before. It's a vision that is cutting edge."

I was very interested to hear what Ken had come up with. He was a marketing genius. I waited for him to tell me his idea and hoped he'd include me in it.

"What if we had a couple, a man and a woman, posing together onstage?" He said. "They'd display the true artistry and creative side of bodybuilding. We'd choreograph the posing routine to music, with synchronized transitions, of course, from pose to pose, showing the beauty of their muscles. I believe it could be the future of the sport. What do you think?"

What did I think? Had Ken lost his mind? I personally thought it was a terrible idea and tried not to show it on my facial expression. Mixed couples? Bodybuilding was a men's sport. Sounded like Ken had gone overboard this time.

"I don't know, Ken. That sounds very risky."

"What do you mean?" He asked.

"There's never been a female posing with a man before."

Ken frowned, then said, "I think you should seriously consider it."

Me? I didn't realize he had me in mind when he told me about his proposal. I was very reluctant to say much. "Well," I said slowly, not wanting to let him down when he'd been so nice to me, "I guess I could do it. It's only an exhibition, right? Who do you have in mind for the female?"

"I have the perfect lady. Lisa Lyon."

"You mean little Lisa, who trains here every day?"

I was surprised. I thought he'd have the current Women's Physique champion, Laura Combs, in mind. I'd never paid Lisa much attention when she was at the gym. But, on occasion I'd seen her talking to some of the other members, though. She was a looker, a petite brunette with a shapely muscular body. Maybe it could work as an extra attraction for the show.

"Yes, Lisa. She's one tough, strong young lady," replied Ken. "She's a Japanese fencing expert, it's called *kendo.* You won Mr. L.A. last year and you're the current Mr. America. You and Lisa are a good match aesthetically. She's around 5'4", weighs around 120 lbs., your stats and hers fit well together. If anyone can do it, it's you guys."

I went home that night with my head still buzzing with Ken's new idea. I'd never seen nor heard anything about a couples routine. It was kind of revolutionary, and I wasn't too keen to have to start creating a routine with another person, let alone a female. But after Ken told me that Lisa was on board with the idea, and that he knew how artistic and creative she was, I dismissed my doubts and decided to give it a try.

When Lisa arrived at the gym we talked and agreed to get together and begin practice sessions that same evening. At 7 p.m. we started to exchange ideas for posing, and after five grueling hours in front of the mirror creating and perfecting a routine, we were satisfied. My uncertainty had been swept away and I began to realize that Ken was indeed a genius. I could see the potential of the event that could turn into an amateur competition in the future.

"I think this is a work of art," I told Lisa, feeling excited. "We're going to blow their minds, especially when they see the contrast of our skin tones - mine's black, yours white. It'll be two muscular bodies in motion. While the audience is listening to the sounds of a live saxophonist playing at the back of the stage."

"Great idea," she said. "And I love the plan that the stage will be completely dark with only two spotlights, giving the routine a real artistic flair. Okay, how about spending a couple of hours each day rehearsing? I'm such a perfectionist."

"I agree, me too." I said. "Our posing routine must be perfect. Without question, I hope this routine will dispel all of the stereotypes of the notion that bodybuilders are simply a bunch of muscle heads. Ken's idea of us posing together allows us to show the pure art form of bodybuilding. Maybe, now, we can help bring the sport out of the dark ages and into the forefront of athleticism and artistic expression through the human body."

Lisa seemed surprised at my insightful comment.

"Speak it out loud, my friend," she said as we prepared to leave the gym. "It's music to my ears. You're deep. You definitely have a gift to share with the world."

CHAPTER 34

Two weeks later, after my intense posing rehearsals with Lisa, we drove to the Embassy auditorium. I was quiet, wondering how the crowd would react. I was anxious to turn pro and hoped this performance wouldn't upset the system. I felt nervous, but at the same time I felt pretty sure we were prepared to perform because we had rehearsed extremely hard.

We waited backstage, Lisa flexing her biceps and me completing a set of push-ups. We heard the emcee address the audience.

"Ladies and gentlemen, coming to the stage next are our guest posers. They will be performing a couples presentation."

Even the emcee sounded unsure of himself. He'd never had to make such an announcement. At his introduction there were a great deal of grumbling from the full house of hard-core spectators. Clearly, they'd never heard of couples posing before, either, and they must have been impatient for the bodybuilding show to begin.

We entered the stage wearing matching shiny red posing suits and took up our positions center stage. On cue the two spotlights shined brightly down upon us, as the auditorium went pitch dark. Lisa glanced over at me. "Are you ready?" She asked.

As my doubts instantly vanished I replied, "I'm ready. Let's have some fun!"

The saxophone player began his solo, a passionate love ballad, and we went into our routine, transitioning gracefully from one classic pose to another. The audience was abnormally quiet. It was eerie. They weren't even talking. Were they waiting for this thing to end so they could get on with the show they'd paid to see? There was no way to gauge if they liked us or not. Lisa and I performed our poses as creatively and beautifully as we'd practiced. Without air conditioning for some unexpected reason on this particular evening, the auditorium became acutely hot and it felt as if the place was ready to explode. You could feel tension in the air. The lack of the audience response led me to wonder if I'd made the right decision to have undertaken such an uncertain proposition. At the very moment that Lisa and I completed our performance everyone stood on their feet in a standing ovation, cheering and applauding. Lisa and I looked at each other and smiled. We were a success! Ken had done it again with his brilliant new endeavor.

The accolades persisted for more than five minutes as we remained onstage thanking them.

A reporter and camera crew from Channel 6 News were waiting to interview us. The reporter shaking his head in amazement, he turned to me saying, "I've never seen anything like your mesmerizing performance! It was absolutely sensational! Whose idea was this?"

"First and foremost," I replied, "I would like to congratulate all of the competitors here today on a job well done. I won this show last year, and it was no easy task. The L.A. show carries a lot of prestige. To answer your question, the concept was Ken Sprague's. He's the owner of Gold's Gym in Santa Monica. Lisa and I were a little apprehensive in the beginning because it had never been done before. But, with a little convincing, we embraced the notion. We appreciate and trust the arts, and most importantly, Lisa and I trust each other. We figured this was the perfect platform to express our creativity. We hope it will serve as a benchmark for the future of couples competition here in the U.S. and hopefully around the world. We can imagine an amateur and possibly a professional division Grand Prix tour in the future. We believe that the general public can relate to and appreciate couples bodybuilding."

The news reporter turned to my partner. "Lisa, you and Tony will go down in history as true pioneers in the sport. What is it that intrigues you about bodybuilding, and what does it feel like to be the first female to flex your muscles here with Tony onstage?"

"There's nothing like it! It felt like freedom, powerful, and sexy at the same time," she told him. "I've always been an athlete and worked out my whole life. Bodybuilding is a perfect transition. I'm very much into the arts. Training with weights allows me to sculpt my body." She flexed her biceps to enormous cheers and applauds. "When a woman is strong, it's exciting," she continued. "It also builds confidence. It is time for women to step out of the shadows and get involved in exercising to better themselves mentally and physically."

"I couldn't agree with you more!" Said the Channel 6 reporter, who then turned to the camera to address his viewers. "Ladies and gentlemen, to completely appreciate what we have witnessed here this evening, you would've had to be here in person. With the compelling standing ovation that these two fine athletes received, I am convinced that couples posing is destined to be the wave of the future. Tony and Lisa gave a gutsy performance that can never be imitated or duplicated." He turned back to us. "We here at Channel 6 thank you guys for an incredible, history-making moment."

Lisa and I thanked him, waved to the audience, and walked offstage. As a result of our performance, Lisa would be crowned by the media as "*The first lady of bodybuilding.*"

The next day I fully realized what the reporter had said about what we had accomplished, thanks to Ken. It was true. The event would happen much sooner than later. In the following year, 1980, this event would be introduced into the sport. It became known as the IFBB Pro World Mixed Pairs Championship.

Although Lisa and I did not partner up again, she went on to win the first International Federation of Body Building (IFBB) Women's World Pro Bodybuilding Championship later in the same year. Subsequently, she modeled; authored fitness books; made the cover of several national and international magazines; and appeared on multiple TV talk shows, crowning her career with the induction into the IFBB Hall of Fame in 2000.

CHAPTER 35

With my full attention focused on my career, that meant that I was neglecting my relationship. Thankfully, Mia was far more understanding than I deserved. As soon as I got back home after the posing exhibition with Lisa, I made a special effort to have a romantic evening with her. We went down to the beach near the Santa Monica pier and sat on beach towels close to the ocean with the surf gently gushing near our feet. The Pacific was as beautiful as always in the pale orange setting sun. We could hear someone's radio playing classic soul, from R&B singer Minnie Riperton's hit single, "Lovin' You." The lyrics perfectly expressed my love for Mia. And I told her, we kissed, watched the beautiful sunset and snuggled close before going back to my studio apartment.

Early the next morning, the phone rang as I was still half asleep. I sat on the side of the bed to answer it. A voice I didn't recognize said, "Hello, Mr. Pearson. My name is Marcel Ruiz. We are presenting a bodybuilding show, the Mr. Belize championship, in Belize, Central America. We'd like to invite you for a guest appearance. The show is a month away. The problem we're having is that we are a small local show and it isn't sanctioned by the IFBB. Would that be an issue for you?"

I told Marcel I wasn't sure, and would call him back.

Maybe it would be okay if I accepted his offer. I could sure use the money. He'd asked me to let him know as soon as possible because of the advertising deadlines. I promised I'd phone him back the next day.

As soon as I hung up I called my first trainer, George Turner, back in St. Louis. I could picture him at his desk going over some workout plans, or flinging swear words at a member.

"George, it's Tony. How are you?"

"Hell, I couldn't be better. I'm getting ready for a show. We got the Masters coming up. Those assholes think I'm done, but I'm never done." He hadn't changed a bit, I was relieved to hear. "Oh, by the way, congratulations on your win."

"Thanks, George. Do you remember all those squat sessions? I guess they paid off in the end, ha! I know you were in Cincinnati at the evening show because, in spite of five thousand spectators cheering their heads off, I could hear your voice clearly when I was standing in the line-up onstage. You were saying, 'Kick their fucking asses, Tony!'" I began to laugh again at the memory, and told him I appreciated him for showing up.

"I couldn't miss it," he said. "How's it going out there?"

"Not too good, George. I know you warned me it'd be tough. Have you seen the latest Weider's *Muscle Builder and Power* magazine that just came out? There's an article in there ripping me apart. It's titled, 'Pearson wins, but... whose t-shirt did Santa wear.' The writer is implying that the show was fixed, that I'm the worst Mr. America ever, and that I'm not deserving of the title. I picked up the magazine and read a portion of the article. 'Suffice it to say that this will go down in bodybuilding history as the most controversial Mr. America to date.' Then it goes on to say, 'you just won't believe how many calls we have received from around the country at the Weider's International Headquarters expressing their outrage with the results of the show.' In another magazine, a different writer commented, "He dreamed of bodybuilding honors. He could hardly wait to come to California to train among the superstars. Little did he know that achievement of his dream would make him, "the unhappiest Mr. America." and listen to this George, next week the Chairman of the AAU along with the judges are flying me down to Austin, Texas, for a meeting to discuss how they can strip me of the title. It's been months since the show and since then I've gotten no contract offers or exhibitions, not to mention being ostracized by the members of Gold's Gym. The IFBB seems determined to prevent me from making a living. My dream of becoming Mr. America has turned into a complete nightmare!"

I was disheartened, and I know he could hear it in my voice. "George, I'm just a kid from the Midwest. I only want to compete! I can't understand why they don't want me. Sounds like the story of my life, I thought to myself. I guess they're hoping I'll go away, but I'm not going anywhere. I just need to figure out an alternative plan."

"I told you, kid, it's a cruel fucking world out there. I know you're tough. They knock you down, you better get the fuck up and fight. I've taught you that much."

"You did, and I'm not going to quit. But one of the reasons I called, George, is for your advice. I got a phone call from Belize to make a guest appearance at their show. It's not sanctioned by the IFBB. Do you think I should go?"

George was silent for a moment, then said, "That's a tough call. But you can't sit there and starve the fuck to death. I suggest you get off your ass and get on down there and make some fucking money."

I told George he was right, that I would accept the Belize offer. I thanked him, and said I would try to visit St. Louis really soon.

My focus returned to the summons to Texas to meet with the Mr. America judges about the controversial judging between me and Ron Teufel at the Mr. America competition.

When I arrived at the hotel conference room on the mezzanine floor for what seemed to me like my murder trial, I was extremely uneasy. The public and press were barred from attending. The judges who had decided the Mr. America contest were all present. At least four of the seven looked like they worked out and were probably former or even current body-builders. I seated myself in the back, the only African-American person in the room. Judges in the bodybuilding industry were all Caucasians so this was the norm to me. Despite that, I was terrified. I'm sure it showed on my face. Pretty soon the chair-man of the AAU, Amateur Athletic Union, came to the podium.

"Gentlemen," he said, "thank you for attending on such short notice. I'd like to thank Tony Pearson, too, for being here. We want to express our sincere apology, Tony, as this inquiry has no ill will toward you personally. I've called this emergency meeting for the sole purpose of discussing the unfortunate in-cident that occurred at the Mr. America contest. The press and fans are outraged at the outcome of the show. We've never been put in such an awkward position in the history of the contest. The press are attacking us with a vengeance, demanding a rever-sal of the results, and asking us to give the title to Ron Teufel. I'm not sure if you've seen the recent article in the *Muscle Builder and Power* magazine. They're calling Mr. Pearson the worst Mr. America ever!"

I winced inwardly when I heard that. It hurt. But I kept my expression impassive as he continued, "We're here today, gentlemen, to determine if we have valid grounds to strip Mr. Pearson of his title. I would like each judge to elaborate on how they judged the show. We will begin with judge number one."

Judge #1: "This is a very subjective sport. We did the best we could. Personally, I judged expertly on what I was seeing on-stage. Teufel for me definitely pulled it out."

The chairman thanked him, and called on the next judge.

Judge #2: "This was one of the most competitive shows ever. In my opinion, any one of the competitors in the top six could have won. I am confident in my decision voting for Mr. Teufel."

Judge #3: "I judged Teufel two weeks earlier at the USA's. I felt he peaked perfectly but then at the Mr. America he seemed to me a little flat and over-dieted. I gave my vote to Mr. Pearson."

"Judge number #4 please," said the chairman.

Judge #4: "There's no discussion that Mr. Pearson won his class. That is not the issue. In my opinion, in the pose down he out-worked Teufel. When it's that close, it comes down to who's willing to outwork the other guy. I felt Mr. Pearson deserved my vote."

Judge #5: "For me, it's the preference of body types. I feel that Mr. Pearson aesthetically had a slight edge. He was in good condition, and he out-posed Ron. But, Teufel in my point of view was slightly bigger in size and his shape was superb. That's why I gave him my vote."

Judge #6: "Teufel was a little off, which left the door open. I believe we all judged the show fairly to the best of our abilities. From my perspective Mr. Pearson deserved to win."

And so it went. Three judges favored Teufel. Only one judge left. Oh my God, this was unbelievably nerve-racking. The chairman asked Judge #7 to explain his viewpoint.

Judge #7: "This was the toughest line-up ever seen on an AAU posing platform. Numerous veteran AAU officials would agree. Pearson won by being a master at his presentation. He was undoubtedly unmatched among the entire field of competitors in terms of his conditioning."

I waited for the chairman to take the podium again and give his verdict. The chairman with a straight-faced expression responded.

"Thank you all for your honesty and for your input concerning this sensitive matter. In my belief all of you gentlemen did an excellent job. In conclusion," -- and here I held my breath -- "I find it virtually impossible to strip Mr. Pearson of his title. At this point, what's done is done. We must move forward. Once again I would like to thank all of you for attending on such short notice. And thank you, Tony, again for attending as well. This meeting is adjourned."

I didn't know whether to laugh or cry as I wiped the sweat from my brow and tried to exhale. I felt exultant at the outcome and knew I could hold my head up high. I had won fair and square. Four of the judges said so and were backed up by the AAU chairman.

I flew back to Los Angeles with a much lighter heart than when I'd left. But fate had another challenge for me.

CHAPTER 36

I called Marcel and gave him the okay to proceed, telling him I'd fly down to Belize as soon as he needed me. I didn't have to wait long. A couple of weeks later I arrived at Goldson International Airport and boarded the shuttle to the hotel that the contest promoter, Marcel, had booked me into. He met me in the lobby, and I liked him immediately. As we shook hands, I was called to the front desk and handed a telegram.

Maybe this was a good-luck wish from George Turner, or the guys at Gold's Gym, I thought. Was I ever wrong! I handed it to Marcel, who read it aloud.

"If you make an appearance tomorrow you will be suspended for life from the International Federation of Body Building. Signed, The President of the IFBB, Ben Weider."

I was stunned and felt sick at my stomach. This was horrible. Being barred from any IFBB competitions meant my career would be over without me even getting into the pro ranks. This was a very small local show. Why were the Weiders so against me, what have I ever done? I just couldn't understand why this was happening to me.

Marcel's face was ashen. "Wow, Mr. Pearson. It seems like we have a problem. What're we going to do now?"

"It's a huge problem," My face showed my disappointment, then I said. "But I have made a commitment to you and I am going to honor it. Don't worry, Marcel, I'll be onstage."

I knew that the advertising for his show had gone out and I was featured prominently on the posters, flyers, and press releases to the local media.

The next evening I was backstage, pumping up, preparing for my performance. I heard the emcee introducing me after the competition portion was completed.

"Ladies and gentlemen, this young man is from the U.S.A. His aesthetics, his performance, and his incredible conditioning earned him three national titles last year. This twenty-two-year-old is the current AAU Jr. Mr. USA, Jr. Mr. America, and Mr. America. Please give him a warm welcome to...Tony Pearson!"

I came onstage to tremendous applauds and cheers as they chanted my name "Tony! Tony!" I went into my posing routine, and as I transitioned from one to another the audience got louder and louder. It was gratifying to hear their response, and I gave it everything I had.

The next day, the flight back to Los Angeles was a very scary one. The pilot had problems with the landing gear. After circling around for the third time we came in for a landing. We were told to put our heads between our legs and prepare for a crash landing. The passengers were horrified, screaming and crying. I defied the order. I sat upright stoically staring straight ahead, feeling no fear. Looking back, I'd asked myself a thousand times what the hell was I thinking? Perhaps, with the way I was raised, I was unable to find my emotional self. I guess the situation was a prelude to the turbulent circumstances of what would come.

I had a few hundred dollars in my pocket from the Belize show, money I desperately needed. I was grateful to Marcel for the opportunity and was somewhat aware of the damage I'd caused myself with the IFBB, but going to Belize was a crucial decision.

I knew the suspension could hurt me but I had no clue of

how much. My emotional state was at its lowest ever. After all the hard work, time and effort I'd put into getting to the top, it had all slipped away in the blink of an eye.

Working out seemed to be the only way to maintain my sanity and of course, my shape. It was my escape from the torture I was feeling inside. I had no clear direction on what to do next.

But the suspension wasn't my only problem. Mia blindsides me. She told me she was resentful of the time I spent on my career. I couldn't blame her. It was true that I was focused completely on bodybuilding. I wanted to be the best in the world and that meant I'd become consumed. I was always at the gym or working at my security jobs. My weekends with her were almost non-existent.

"You wake up every day," she said, "and go to the gym, come home, and eat and sleep. You never want to have fun anymore. What's happened to us?"

I knew this was serious and I didn't have much of an answer. She was right, of course. Still, I went on the defensive and tried to calm her down by taking her in my arms, but she pushed me away.

"We do have fun, baby. I thought you liked working out," I said.

"I like going to the gym because it's exciting, but there's more to life than that. It isn't everything. You're so obsessed with becoming a pro. That's not a real sport anyway!" She shouted, "You are never going to enjoy your life. Baby, I love you, but I feel I don't have all of you. I need more." She began to cry. "You've got to decide if you want to be with me, cause I don't want to compete with bodybuilding anymore. I've tried. This is your dream, not mine. You're never going to quit."

"Baby, c'mon, you know how I feel about you," I sorrowfully said. "It's not fair to make me choose. I love you, and I don't want to lose you. I'm sorry if I haven't been giving you the attention you deserve. Lately, I've been dealing with a lot of stress. You don't understand. I'm sorry if I make you feel that way, that's not my intention."

"This isn't easy for me," she painfully uttered. "I love you with every fiber of my being, but this isn't for me. Maybe the timing is off. Why couldn't we have met later in life? I'm only twenty! I just want to have fun, live my life, and be free."

I began pleading with her, teary-eyed. I felt terrible.

"Baby, how am I going to live without you? You're breaking my heart. Please don't leave me like this."

She dropped her head and said, "I just can't do it anymore. I'm sorry. You know I'll always love you."

She looked into my eyes, came close, gave me a long hug, and walked out the door. I stood in the middle of the floor flabbergasted, then sat down on the bed with my head in my hands. Her leaving would haunt me.

My depression lasted what seemed like forever. But eventually, somehow, mentally I'd pick up the pieces and force myself to keep going. Soon thereafter, I received a phone call from a promoter in Providence, Rhode Island. He invited me to make a guest appearance at one of his shows being held in two weeks' time. I agreed. I got myself together and really stepped up my training. Due to my poor man's diet of tuna fish and water and my fast metabolism, I got in shape fairly quickly.

When I arrived at the auditorium it was filled with two thousand on-lookers. I had the jitters because this was only my third appearance since winning the Mr. America title, but the moment I hit my first pose to the music from the movie soundtrack "Shaft," all my fears disappeared. My posing was a great success. As I came off the stage a young man expressed how amazing I looked and said I should enter the WBBG, Mr. World competition in New York City within a week's time. (I always made it a priority to appear in top shape at any event) He offered to drive me there. I said okay. I was excited at this unexpected situation. It was forcing me back into the fight. I went to the local gym and trained extremely hard for the next week.

The guy kept his promise and drove me to New York for the contest. Backstage, I pumped up in the weight room area along with all the other competitors, wondering if after so many months away from competing had affected my competitive spirit. Onstage, I stared nervously into the crowd along with the other finalists while we waited anxiously for the results. The head judge handed the emcee the scores. The emcee spoke into the microphone.

"Ladies and gentlemen, the winner, of the 1979 Professional Mr. World is...Tony Pearson!"

I was ecstatic. To actually win the title was an incredible, emotional moment. Then I found out later that night that I'd also won a trip to compete in the 1979 NABBA Amateur Mr. Universe competition in London, England.

CHAPTER 37

I had arrived back in Venice. Even though I'd done my best to move forward after my break-up with Mia, my feeling for her was still deeply embedded into my heart. I just couldn't get her out of my mind. Every girl that somehow resembled her brought back such heartfelt memories of her. The intense pain of losing her came rushing back as if we'd just broken up yesterday. I was on the Venice boardwalk headed to the weight pen for my daily routine workout, although I didn't feel like it. It was cold and overcast, matching my gloomy mood.

I could hear a stereo playing loudly in one of the upstairs apartments. It was a Chi-Lites song, "Have You Seen Her?" Perfect. My mood shifted to dreadful. I zipped up my sweat jacket and put my hands into my pockets as I stared at the ground. When I looked up I saw my friend, Robby Robinson, approaching with his usual swagger. He was always smiling and I admired him for his positive outlook on life and his cool temperament.

"Robby, how are you?"

"T.P.!" He always called me by my initials. "I'm great. What's going on with you? I see you've been walking around lately with your head down in the dumps."

"It's Mia, remember her?"

"Yeah," he said. "I used to see you guys at the gym."

"She broke up with me. She gave me an ultimatum. It's either her or bodybuilding. I love her so much, I don't know what to do. I'm walking around in a fog. I'm going out of my mind."

Robby looked me straight at me. This time he wasn't smiling. "Look at you, feeling sorry for yourself! You came out here from St Louis with nothing in your pockets, fighting for a better life, which we all know is no joke here in L.A. Only the strong survive. Don't let that girl get you down. She's young. There'll be someone else that's going to respect and support what you're trying to achieve.

What are you going to do, fight or give up? What you need to do T.P. is pick your head up, man. Stick your chest in the air and remember the real purpose of why you came out here."

Robby's speech resonated with me. He was right. My dream, my vision was still out there. I was living the beginning of it. I had to keep going. I thanked him, telling him his advice meant a lot to me.

But that was easier said than done. Okay, I told myself that losing Mia was something I could handle on my own, but the Ben Weider decision was out of my control. I needed to seek the advice of a guy who might know the answer better than anyone else.

A few days later I was very agitated when I went over to Kent's apartment. He'd been my great friend and supporter ever since I met him. He'd noticed Arnold was my mentor. Moreover, Kent saw how disciplined I'd been when it came to my workouts and competing. I think he respected my disposition. I enjoyed talking with him, especially about bodybuilding. But now I felt so depressed I could barely think straight.

When I'd arrived he welcomed me into his home. He'd been watching television. He switched it off as I took a seat at the dining table. Kent sat on the large sectional sofa, asking me what was up and saying that I hadn't looked too happy these days.

"Mia broke up with me," I said, not even glancing at him as

I spoke. "But that's the least of my problems. I have a much bigger one that I hope you can help me with."

"Sure, buddy, calm down. What the hell is going on?"

"I've been suspended from the IFBB for life!"

"What?" Kent was astonished. "That's unbelievable. What happened?" He asked.

"I needed to make some money. I'm having a tough time making a living." I was so distraught I could hardly get the words out telling the story of the promoter from Belize, the local show there, and the telegram from Ben Weider.

Kent came over and patted my shoulder. "Take it easy, kid, I know. Well, if you are under suspension it leaves the door open for other opportunities. This means you are allowed to compete in other federations in Europe and make guest appearances there. What else can you possibly do under the circumstances?"

"Europe?" I perked up a little. "Wow, I've never thought of that. I guess you're right. I knew you would know what to do. You always seem to have an answer to my complicated life. I'm still learning how things work."

I got up to leave. Kent saw me to the door, saying. "Keep your head up. I know you're torn up about Mia, but you've got to let it go. I'm sure there'll be another girl just around the corner."

Kent proved correct. I did meet another lovely young lady, Mary Forte, at the bodybuilding event in Rhode Island where I guest posed a few months earlier. We kept in touch in the meantime. She was in her early twenties and came from Trinidad. I was intrigued with her soft-spoken French accent. She had a three-year-old daughter, Ney-Ney from a previous relationship. As Mary told it, it was love at first sight with us. True, but I was a little apprehensive because of the distance and wanting to take it slowly after Mia. But after getting to know her better through letters and phone calls, all of that changed. We had a long distance relationship for a while and she and the baby Ney-Ney decided to move across the country to live with me.

A couple of weeks after Mary and the baby had moved in we had to leave my studio and move into a dilapidated one-bedroom apartment farther in-land from the beach in Venice.

Despite having a beautiful little family now who loved me, I was still in despair. As the weeks went by, I felt worse than ever. I had no ambition anymore. While I had some accomplishments with other federations, they weren't recognized by the IFBB. Until you'd achieved a level of success in the IFBB, you are not taken seriously. It seems as if you are on the outside looking in. In my case with a life suspension hanging over my head, it was agonizing knowing that this dream that I'd worked so hard for had been all for naught. I was so young and naïve. I'd chased that elusive something that doesn't exist. I had allowed myself to become disillusioned with the sport. Everything I thought I knew and believed was shattered. The rejection by the establishment and humiliation by the press took an awful toll on my sense of worth. There didn't seem to be any hope left. I'd reached bottom.

One morning when Mary and the baby had gone off to the market I was unable to handle my depression any longer. I stumbled into the bathroom, took out a couple of bottles of sleeping pills and swallowed them all. I staggered into the living room to lay on the sofa but didn't make it. I collapsed onto the floor.

Mary found me there when she returned from shopping. She tried to wake me but I was not responding. She realized that something was ghastly wrong. She half-dragged, half-pushed me to get me into her car and rushed to the hospital Emergency Room.

Minutes later I was transferred to a bed. Mary was completely frantic. She was trembling and sobbing when she gave the doctor the empty bottles. Then she asked, "Doctor, please tell me he's going to be all right?" He didn't answer her. "I can't believe he would want to take his own life!"

Mary heard the doctor tell the nurse to prep me in order to pump my stomach, and she was asked to wait outside. Several minutes later the nurse came out and asked Mary to fill out some paperwork.

"How old is your boyfriend? Any idea why he'd want to take his life?" The nurse asked.

"He's twenty-three," Mary told her. "He's been very depressed lately because of his work. He just keeps saying how the bodybuilding world destroyed his life. He won Mr. America a couple of years ago, and ever since then he's been spiraling down into this horrible depression. He said they broke his spirit, and for a while he didn't want to train or ever compete again. He's made threats a few times to end it all, but I didn't think he meant it. He spends most of his days locked into the bedroom. He's very conflicted. He wants to quit bodybuilding, but it's his only source of income."

As the nurse listened sympathetically, Mary continued while wiping the tears from her eyes "He seemed to be getting a little better lately, but then this happened. Oh God! Is he going to be okay, ma'am?"

Just then, Doctor James walked up and introduced himself to Mary. "Mr. Pearson is under sedation. He's going to pull through."

"Are you sure, doctor?" Mary asked doubtfully.

"We can assure you, Ms. Forte, that he's going to be fine," said the doctor very calmly. "He'll need to stay here for a few days for monitoring. He took a lot of pills, the overdose was a very close call. He's a very lucky young man."

"Thank you, doctor, oh my God, thank you so much! He's

such a gentle soul, but he's been in a lot of pain lately."

Mary went over to the nurse's desk to thank her. The nurse gave her a hug and said, "You know, my husband's a bodybuilder. He used to compete but not at the pro level. Just a few amateur competitions back in the day."

"That's awesome," Mary said.

"Do I hear wedding bells anytime soon?"

Mary replied that we'd talked about it, and promised the nurse if it happened, she'd receive an invite.

CHAPTER 38

I had a very slow recovery from my miserable ordeal. It was about eight months before I'd gotten myself together fully. But thankfully, after rebuilding my strength I was back into serious training again. Several European countries invited me over for guest appearances and I accepted.

One day Serge Nubret called me from his home in Paris. He was around 14 years older, my senior, a 6'0" world champion bodybuilder with a superb physique. We'd become good friends. He came from the French Caribbean island of Guadeloupe and his family relocated to Paris when he was a teen. Serge was in several films, including "Pumping Iron," where he had placed second at the Mr. Olympia. He also acted in French and Italian movies with top stars. He was head of the IFBB in Europe from 1970 to 1975. Whenever I was in Europe we spoke by phone, or met if it was convenient. With his strong French accent he asked me how things were going.

"Hi, Serge. I'm doing well, but I'm a little exhausted with all the training and traveling. You know how challenging it can be."

"Yes, I know. Tony, you are in fantastic shape. I've seen photos of you from your shows. Why don't you stay one more week in Europe and go to London to compete in the NABBA Pro Mr. Universe? You won the amateur WABBA world championship last year and came in second in the NABBA amateur division. How about trying now to win the pro title?"

The NABBA initials stood for the National Amateur Body Building Association, the original contest was founded and based out of London, but their competitions were held in different countries all over the world. WABBA was the World Amateur Body Building Association.

"Wow! Really? I haven't heard anything about the show. I mean, I've been so busy. I believe I'm in good enough shape, but I've been here over a month and my girlfriend back home is expecting me there tomorrow. Let me call her and I'll, um, get right back to you."

I dreaded calling Mary, but this was a chance of a lifetime, a golden opportunity. It could help to propel me back to the top echelon of the bodybuilding world. When I called Mary, she said she and Ney-Ney were in the middle of playing some children's games.

"Hi baby, how're you doing, how's the baby?"

"I'm okay, Ney-Ney is fine, she asks for you every day. You're coming in tomorrow, right?"

"Mary, please don't get upset but I need to stay another week. My friend here thinks I should go to London and compete for Mr. Universe." I held my breath for her reply and it wasn't pretty.

"Tony, you promised me!" I could hear the anger in her voice. She was livid. "It's been over a month! What the hell! I just can't do this anymore."

I made a desperate attempt to show Mary the importance of the situation for going to England.

"Baby, please, just one more week. Can you give me that? I'm doing this for us, it could be a great chance to make a living and be able to support you and Ney-Ney if I win. I'm sure I'll get some endorsements with some supplement companies."

"No, you're not doing this for us, you're doing it for yourself. I'm done with this relationship. You're never going to be finished with this bodybuilding stuff! It's very lonely here without you! I can't live this way, always waiting for you here on my own." The sadness in her voice just killed me. "If you don't come home tomorrow, I swear, I am leaving you!"

"Baby this isn't a hobby. I'm not doing it for me. It's my job! I'm begging you, please, don't make me choose."

Mary was crying and I had no words to comfort her. I was going to London, and I guess she knew I had already made my choice. I asked if there was anything I could say to make her stay. She answered that she'd thought about it a lot over the past month, and now she was done. I told her I loved her, that she was my everything, and to give Ney-Ney a hug and kiss for me. Then I said good-bye. And hung up.

I flew to London with a heavy heart but tried to block it out. I felt pretty good when I arrived at the hotel and found a large crowd of fans waiting for the competitors, asking for autographs and to take photos together. It was the same when I entered the auditorium the next evening. It was filled to capacity with six thousand viewers from all over the world, including the U.S.A.

I was flexing back-stage, waiting to walk on after the emcee announced my name. I was the first contestant.

"Ladies and gentlemen," the emcee, said with his formal British accent, "Welcome to the 32nd annual NABBA Mr. Universe. This year we have a sensational lineup of twenty-six international athletes from twenty different countries. We're in for a really exciting evening. Our first competitor in the professional category, from the United States of America is...Tony Pearson!"

The fans began chanting "Tony! Tony! Tony!" I had a sudden flashback to the cotton field of Mississippi and the chanting of my name I'd heard as a little child. It was an awfully sad moment, a moment of grief as the vision of myself with that huge cotton sack around my body filled my mind and Auntie Bettie hitting me in the back of my head. I came back to earth as the emcee repeated my name. I made my way onto the stage, taking the center spot and began my routine, fighting every inch of the way in the hopes of winning, performing to "Shaft" from the movie soundtrack.

The audience continued its cheering and applauding, shouting out my name again, and "USA! USA!" Two minutes later I had completed my routine. Within an hour and a half all of the other contestants had finished their performances. The head judge handed the emcee the names of the three finalists. American, Dave Johns, Ian Lawrence from England, and myself. We appeared back onstage. The head judge told us to spread out and give ourselves some room. When the upbeat music began, he instructed, "Pose down!"

I forcefully went into my poses, determined to give it everything I had. I'd rehearsed so much as I hit my marks, transitioning from one pose to another with a smoothness that I'd hoped for. I was concentrating so hard I almost didn't hear the signal to stop.

We could hear the BBC Sports announcer shouting into his microphone above the lively crowd, "Ladies and gentlemen, what an incredible battle we have between these final three competitors for the overall title. Pearson is very aggressive, going right after Johns, hitting various devastating most muscular shots. Turning to the back, hitting multiple back poses and finishing up with his famous vacuum crushing abdominal pose. He repeats them over and over. My goodness, this is epic!"

The announcer paused for a second, then continued, "Johns is fighting back tooth and nail, hitting double biceps and side chest poses. Lawrence is coming on strong against them, flexing with ferocious intensity, throwing every pose imaginable. Oh my God! This is such a spectacular turn of event to witness. What a serious fight we have here this evening. The crowd is out of control, on their feet, screaming their heads off. This has to be the best pose down since the beginning of the Mr. Universe contest, dating back to the late forties."

The head judge spoke into the microphone, thanking us, and giving us the cue to stop. Then he indicated there would be a few minutes' pause to allow the judges to select the winner. No longer than a minute later, the head judge revealed that they had "made a decision."

He handed the results to the emcee, who announced, "Ladies and gentlemen, here are the results." He paused. "In third place, from England... Ian Lawrence."

The audience really went crazy cheering for their countryman.

"In second place, from the USA... Dave Johns. And, the winner of the 1980 Professional Mr. Universe, from the USA is... Tony Pearson!"

There was a passionate loud uproar in the audience as they cheered and applauded. The victory platform had been set up after we finished our pose down, and I took my place in the middle of the other two competitors. I was presented with the trophy, which I then placed at my feet. I raised both arms in victory, a great smile covered my face. I'd won! I shed tears of joy but there was also deep sadness. My victory was bitter-sweet as it had cost me Mary and Ney-Ney.

The BBC announcer, very proper in a black suit and tie, was waiting backstage to interview me.

"Mr. Pearson," he said in his formal British accent, "last year you definitely put up an unforgettable fierce battle, placing a very close second to Ahmet Enunlu of Turkey in the amateur division. Now you return to capture the professional title. How does that make you feel?"

"It's unbelievable, it's like the greatest moment of my life. I'm overjoyed with the win. Coming from a painful childhood to this point there's no words to truly, express everything I'm feeling. A week ago I was ready to fly back to the states. Today, I've finally done it. I just wished Mary and the baby Ney-Ney could be here to share this victory with me." Tears begin to trickle slowly down my cheeks.

"How old are you?" Asked the announcer.

"Twenty-three." I said as I fought to gather my composure.

"I'm sure there are lots of young, up-and-coming bodybuilders who look up to you. Who was your idol growing up?"

"My first idol," I said, "was heavyweight boxing champion Muhammad Ali. I was very young at the time I met him, but I've never forgotten the encounter when he shook my hand."

"Is it true you were discovered by Arnold Schwarzenegger?"

"Yes. When I was nineteen and just starting out at Muscle Beach. I became inspired and driven, as he told me I had potential to be a champion." I've never forgotten those words and they still resound in my ears to this day.

"For those fans who see you in the magazines and onstage, perhaps they think they know you. My question is, who is Tony Pearson?"

I didn't hesitate in my reply. "I'm just a down-to-earth type of guy. What you see is what you get. I'm kind of an introvert, a perfectionist, goal-oriented."

"When you're not training, what do you do for fun?"

"I love the movies, going to the beach, and dancing."

"Favorite movie?" He asked.

"'Rocky, for sure. I must have watched Sylvester Stallone's Rocky movie and its sequel a dozen times." I never tire of identifying somewhat with the character and his story.

The BBC announcer asked me another interesting question. "You're a great performer, Mr. Pearson. Does that come naturally or do you have to work at it?"

"No, it's a lot of work. It's a very big part of my training. I believe how you present your physique on stage is essential."

Then he asked how long I planned to compete. I told him until I was sixty or seventy. "Bodybuilding is a lifestyle." I added.

My next contest, he asked? "I haven't thought about it. I just want to make it home and rest-up, then decide."

I'd hoped that Mary had changed her mind and would be there when I arrived. I'd thought we were the perfect little family. But I guess all the time away was too much and she couldn't bear the thought of living in uncertainties. I missed them a lot when I was on the road, but my career took precedence.

CHAPTER 39

I came home to an empty apartment. Mary had taken all of her and Ney-Ney's belongings, of course, and the place felt as if the life had been sucked out of it. The silence was acutely distressing. I set the beautiful base and the crystal glass trophy down on the floor, threw my suitcase and gym bag into the bedroom, and turned on the television in the living room.

When I sat on the sofa and casually looked underneath one of the chairs at our small dining table, I saw a furry gray toy elephant that Ney-Ney had left behind. I picked it up, and tears came afresh. My emotions were raw and my heart was saddened at my loss.

After the euphoria of the London win had worn off, life had returned back to normal, though things had slowed down quite a bit more than I'd expected. I had no invites for seminars or guest appearances from the other federations. Movie extra work helped a little along with my new security job. It took a lengthy amount of time before I could come to terms with the break-up with Mary. I knew in my heart it was time to let go and to move on. Several months later my friends from the beach suggested that I join them one evening at a Cuban-American restaurant.

During the dinner I observed a really cute young lady sitting at the table opposite us. She was facing me. I noticed that when she engaged in conversation with her girlfriend, she kept glancing my way. We made eye contact. She was very attractive and she smiled at me once or twice. I took that as a sign. I had to meet her. Sharon Smith and I exchanged phone numbers, and soon we were dating. She was biracial Caucasian and Cuban, and she was in her early twenties. I've always been attracted to petite women, and she was just my type. She was very bright, outgoing, and lovable. I felt blessed to have met someone like her. We enjoyed a deep relationship and fit together well. One day Sharon and I were having a quiet lunch at home. She was telling me how she had applied to the prestigious accredited liberal arts and sciences program at the American University in Paris, France. But, she didn't think her chances of getting in were good because of all the other applicants from around the world. I told her she could achieve anything that she set her mind to do. I wasn't surprised that she had applied. I felt she was destined to have a great future ahead of her.

Just then I heard a knock at the door. Sharon was closer and she went to answer it. When she opened the door there were two Los Angeles Police officers standing there.

"Can I help you?" She said.

"Does Tony Pearson live here?"

"Yes."

"May I ask who you are?" Asked one of the officers. "I'm Sharon, his girlfriend."

"We were sent here by his sister, Carolyn Pearson. We need to speak to him."

My sister? What could have happened to bring the police to my door? I was completely out of touch with my family at this point, even with Carolyn, but obviously she had tracked me down once again. I approached the officers. "Yes, sir," I said.

"How can I help you?"

"We're here to inform you that your dad has died," he stated as they turned and suddenly left.

Dad died? It felt like someone had punched me in the stomach. It was the furthermost thing I could imagine. He was a tough guy, an ex-con who survived prison and a couple of attempts on his life. A wife abuser and a child abuser. A man who I thought would live forever. I was in shock. I turned to Sharon. "Sharon, oh my God! I'm lost for words. I can't think right now."

Sharon expressed her sympathy. "Baby, I'm sorry. Please take my hand, and come sit down. I don't know what to say."

"There's nothing you can say, baby." I said. "The sad thing is, I can't afford to go home for the funeral. I've barely got bus fare to go across town. God! I feel numb. I remember the last time I was in Memphis a few years ago. When I went to visit him he was his regular mean self. He criticized me the whole time about lifting weights, said I should be looking for a job instead."

Sam Pearson with Carolyn's son, 1975

Sharon hugged me as I continued, "This might sound kind of weird but when I was ending my visit with him I had a premonition. I started to cry, and a feeling of deep sorrow came over me as I knew it would be the last time I ever saw him. Oh, God, Sharon, I'm starting to feel sick, like I'm going to throw up. This is hitting me hard and I don't know why. There was no love lost between us that's for sure."

I had never told Sharon, or my other girlfriends, about my

upbringing as a child. I was still secretive about it, but I'm sure they sensed that my family didn't play an important part in my life as I never mentioned my parents or other relatives. Sometimes I'd mention Carolyn but that was the extent of it.

Now, though, I felt like sharing my feelings with Sharon because she was so understanding and caring. "Of all the despicable things I'd heard about him, how abusive he was to everyone, especially my mom, I can't figure out why I am feeling this grief now that he's gone."

People usually grieve for the passing of someone they loved, someone who meant a great deal to them, unlike the deplorable person my dad was.

Sharon did her best to comfort me. "It's your dad, and no matter what, there will always be a bond. He's the only dad you've got. Maybe you were hoping subconsciously that you'd have a chance to reconnect with him on a deeper level. Perhaps, develop a special friendship. I'm sorry, baby. I know how you're feeling because I lost my dad when I was twelve. It's been really hard on me. It'll take a while, but I'm sure you'll find a sense of closure."

I knew she was wrong but I appreciated her compassion. I would never accept my dad's cruel behavior or forgive him for all the pain and suffering he'd caused to so many people, including myself. True, he was the only so-called dad I'll ever have. May his soul rest in peace.

CHAPTER 40

Within a couple of weeks, when Sharon was out visiting friends, I went to see Kent at his apartment. He was watching football with the sound turned up loud. I felt at a loose end and it was always good to spend time with him. His personality was generally upbeat and cheerful.

"Hey, Tony, what's up, buddy? C'mon in and take a seat."

I sat on a stool at the kitchen counter. "I'm doing okay. I'm just kind of hanging out these days." I said.

"Are you hungry? There's some chicken on the stove. I just made it. There's some salad in the fridge, too. Help yourself."

I got a plate from the kitchen cabinet and filled it with chicken and salad. We both watched the game for a while. When a commercial came on Kent said, "So, what are you going to do now? I mean, what are your plans? Your European opportunities seem to have ended. I think you should write a letter of apology to Ben Weider so you can get reinstated back into the IFBB. I'm sure he'll let you back in."

I brightened up. This was a surprise suggestion. "Really? You think so, Kent? They'll take me back?"

"Yeah. I'm sure they will."

"Okay, I'll send him a letter."

I'd expected an immediate reply but it actually took a few weeks to hear back. When I did receive a response, I rushed over to Gold's Gym. It was crowded. Kent was busy at work at the counter checking people in, selling merchandise, and folding T-shirts, all at the same time.

"Kent, you got a minute?" I waved the letter in the air. "Look, it's from the IFBB. It says, 'We're honored to welcome you back into the IFBB federation!' How about that?"

Kent leaned over the counter to me and gave a big smile. "See, I told you. All you had to do was write a letter. So now, my friend, you are officially a member of the IFBB, Mr. Pearson."

I was overly excited. It felt that things were beginning to turn around for me. I was back in the IFBB and eligible to compete in their shows.

A few days later, after my morning workout, I was at the Rose Café near Gold's Gym. Many of us frequented the place, including Arnold who was having breakfast with a few friends. He approached me and suggested that I compete in the IFBB, Mr. Universe contest in Australia in a of couple months. I smiled with excitement, and answered that it was a great idea. "Thanks for inviting me!" I said.

Arnold Schwarzenegger, circa 2005

Later that day, after my security shift was over, I returned to the gym to share the good news with Kent. "Hey Kent, you won't believe it! I ran into Arnold at a café and he invited me to compete in the IFBB Mr. Universe contest in Australia in a couple of months. I'm really looking forward to competing on an IFBB stage for the first time."

Kent's face showed his delight at my good news. "That's terrific, buddy. Just make sure you go down there in shape."

"You know me, you don't have to worry about that. I'll be in the best shape of my life." I said firmly.

CHAPTER 41

The next morning, as I was worrying about finances and getting dressed to go to the gym, Carolyn called. She had gotten my number somehow. She said she was doing great and wanted to know how things were going with my bodybuilding career. "It's been tough, sis, I'm still working hard trying to make things happen."

"Don't worry, little brother. You've got to hang in there and be patient." She said encouragingly.

"How did you get my number?" I asked.

"I have my ways," she said, chuckling. "If I want to find someone, I will."

I smiled and said, "I feel sorry for the guys you date. They can't escape you, ha!"

"You got that right," she answered. We both laughed! I asked Carolyn if she was still living in St. Louis. When she said she was, she asked, "Isn't it time for you to visit your mother?"

It's her mother, too, but she'd always say "your mother." "I know you have mixed emotions about what happened back in those days, but I feel it's something you should take care of. I've been talking to her and I can tell she misses you."

"You know why I haven't gone and how I feel about the whole situation. We've talked about this, Carolyn."

"I know, I know!" She replied.

"I've been hurt and lost for answers as far back as I can remember. It's too painful!"

"Yeah, I'm sure, but, I think it's something you really need to do. There's no pressure from me," Carolyn said. "But please think about it. Here's the address."

Even thinking about traveling back to Memphis as I spoke with Carolyn was bringing up the horror of those days. The pain was still present. But maybe she was right. Perhaps, there was a way to kill the demons, so to speak.

I thought well and hard about my sister's suggestion to visit my mom. Reluctantly, I decided to make the trip. Everybody needs their mom, and I was lucky enough that mine was still living. But I had no idea of the emotional trauma that was to come.

I scraped together enough money for the plane fare and landed at the Memphis International Airport. I made my way to mom's house, holding in my hand the piece of paper I'd written the address Carolyn gave me, and I knocked on the door. After twenty-two years I was finally about to reunite with Mom. It felt surreal. I wasn't even sure I wanted to see her. I was so mixed up I felt almost ill. I began having atrocious flashbacks when I was living in Memphis with my great Auntie Bettie. One in particular as a young child being struck across the face and head with her hand repeatedly. She'd then make me strip down to my underwear and stand in a corner for hours with my arms extended over my head, facing the wall as a way of further punishment. I was paralyzed with fear to move a muscle, knowing if I had she'd have skinned me alive and fed me to the pigs. She ruled the shack with absolute despotism. I watched her drink herself blind while she'd finished one beer and immediately took another. The more she drank the redder her face became as her hot-blooded temper surged out of control. She'd led me to believe how my mom was a disgusting person for running off with another man and leaving all of us kids behind. As I got older I realized the disdain my Auntie had toward my mom. She would fly into rage screaming and yelling, calling her a yellow whore, saying if she ever stepped foot in her yard again she was going to kill her. But now the moment had arrived for me to hear the real truth about what had happened all those many years ago.

An African-American man opened the door. He was much too old to be my brother, Sam, Jr. It didn't matter who he was as I was in somewhat of a trance, sort of. As soon as he led me into the living room I saw my mom. She was standing there looking as nervous as I was. Seems we both felt a level of intense anxiety at this momentous meeting.

"Hi, Mom," I said. "How are you?" I was surprised at how young she looked, how pretty and stylishly dressed she was.

At once she came towards me, arms outstretched, to give me a big hug. We embraced tightly. My uneasiness all of a sudden faded within a few seconds. There was a sense of calmness in the room, as if I'd been with her my whole life.

She broke the embrace to stand back and look at me. "I'm doing good." She replied with her soft voice, the one I remembered. "My, look at all those muscles! We only get to see you on television. You're looking good, son."

"Thanks, Mom."

"Come over here and have a seat on the sofa. You know that Tommy," she said, indicating the guy who opened the door, "has every magazine you've ever been in. He's your biggest fan. Oh, I forgot. You don't know I remarried. It's been twenty years now."

"I know, Carolyn told me. You're in great shape, Mom."

"I've been trying to eat right. Doctor's orders." I could tell the doctor had suggested the diet from the unhappy facial expression she made. "I've been going to the Y.M.C.A to exercise in the pool. I've lost fifteen pounds, but I've got a lot more to go."

"Keep it up. The pool is the best workout for you." I told her. Mom got up from the sofa, took me by the hand and led me into the kitchen where we sat at the kitchen table. It was obvious she felt the most comfortable there and wanted to talk to me seriously and at length. I was a little apprehensive hearing her story. But I sensed Mom needed to get it off her chest. I doubted anything could set the record straight and make me feel better about it all, but as an adult I could see her story from a new point of view.

"I've been waiting for this day for a long, time," she began. "It's been a heavy burden on my shoulders for all these years. You know, you guys were babies. I never wanted to leave you. I prayed to God about what to do, and I heard a voice say, 'You can always get the kids back.' Your dad was so much older than me when we met. I was this young, naive little girl from Mississippi. I didn't know anything about life."

Sounding more and more distressed as she recounted the sad story, my mother stumbled through tears to explain herself. I could see how extremely difficult for her this was. She gave an account of all the times Dad had tortured her and boasted about the man he had killed.

"I was scared to my core. I had no choice but to leave y'all. If I didn't I wouldn't be here today. I want you to know, Tony, how sorry I am. I've had many excruciating nights crying about what happened, and what I was forced to do to save my life. Sam was full of evil. I saw him beating his own mother on several occasions."

She was crying. It was clear she was in tremendous pain describing those dreadful times, and there was nothing I could do to lessen her agony except to love her.

"I know, Mom. Please don't cry. I'm so sorry it all happened. But we all survived, that's what matters. I know you tried your best. We're all blessed we still have you in our lives. I've missed you so much. Give me a hug." She gave me a long hug and then says, "You don't know how much I've missed you, too, son. My little baby, and now look at the fine man you've become. I am so proud of you. I love you." "I love you too, mom." I replied.

Mae Pearson with my Grandfather (her Father), Sandy, and one of her nephews, circa 1950

CHAPTER 42

The Sydney Opera House Auditorium in Australia was everything I could imagine it to be. Facing the harbor, it was one of the most iconic buildings on the planet, its sail-like facade soaring above the bay. The Concert Hall, where the contest was being held, was spectacular and seated two thousand five hundred people. I loved the locals' accents. I was honored to have been invited to take part in the event. I was excited and a bit nervous. This was my first IFBB contest and I had no idea who I'd be up against. The American bodybuilding and Australian media were there in droves, despite the fact there hasn't been any published coverage from the event to date.

I was back-stage definitely feeling the contest jitters as I was warming-up by completing my last set of dips. I'd positioned two chairs across from each other and was using them as a dip bar. I stood up ready to walk onstage, waiting for my name to be announced when a judge approached and unexpectedly pulled me aside and whispered, "You're never going to win." His face was serious and his comments were delivered in a grim tone. "You'll always be in the top five, and you'll always make money."

I was flabbergasted. I'm sure the dismay showed in my face.

"What do you mean, sir?" I asked. "I don't understand. I don't know what to say. We haven't even had tonight's finals yet."

"Just listen to what I said and don't ask questions," he replied.

The judge immediately walked away, leaving me lost for words. What was that all about? A warning, perhaps? Still mystified, I went onstage after the emcee announced all the finalists. The audience was deafeningly loud, cheering and applauding. The head judge, as always, was sitting in front of the stage with the six other judges. He told us to stand in a straight line and we followed his instructions.

"Gentlemen, a quarter turn to the right, please. A quarter turn to the back. Now, face forward with your feet together. Thank you. You can exit the stage, and we'll begin the three finalists' individual routines."

The three of us, Dennis Tinerino, an American, Roger Walker, an Australian, and I, performed our posing routines to the music we'd each chosen for our performances. We were only allowed two minutes and this time I didn't go over the limit. I didn't want to get disqualified in light of what the judge had revealed to me backstage.

Soon thereafter, the head judge announced they had the final placing, and handed the results sheet to the emcee. The other competitors and I stood on stage waiting for the outcome.

"Ladies and gentlemen, in third place... from the USA, Tony Pearson," said the emcee. "In second place, from Australia, is Roger Walker. And the winner, of the 1981 IFBB Pro, Mr. Universe from the USA, is Dennis Tinerino!"

There was a mixture of cheers and boos among the packed house of spectators.

So the judge who had whispered to me was right, at least about this particular contest. I couldn't help but wonder where the fix had come from, if there was one. Well, the show was over. I was trying to hide being disheartened, but it was tough because I knew I was in good shape and my posing I felt was on point. I didn't want to take anything away from Dennis Tinerino. He was a great champion bodybuilder. He'd won Mr. Universe several times, and was viewed as an icon.

This was a gut-wrenching welcoming back into the federation. I packed my bags and I flew home.

On the plane I was at least cheered up a little by the fact that I would have Sharon at my side to share my frustration. She always knew how to comfort me in times of stress. Her showing her love for me was what I desperately needed at the time.

But that was not to be. Sharon was waiting for me at my little apartment. "Baby, I had to see you," she said nervously. "I've got something to tell you. I have some good news and some bad news."

I was sympathetic to whatever it was, although I was feeling let down from the contest. We hugged and sat on the bed. I asked her what happened.

"I know we've only been together for a few months," she said. "But I fell hard for you. You know I love you, right?"

"I know baby, I know. What is it? What are you trying to say?"

"Remember when we first started going together and I mentioned I was waiting to hear back from the arts university in Paris? I forgot all about it but then today I received a letter of acceptance." Sharon began to cry, saying through her tears, "This isn't right. Life is so unfair. Baby, I've got to leave next week."

"Oh, my God," I said.

On top of the Australian debacle, now I was about to lose the woman I loved with all my heart. We had a very special relationship, one I hadn't known could exist. I couldn't imagine life without her. I got emotional, too, and tears filled my eyes.

"What can I say? I'm speechless. I love you. You're the brightest star of my life. You've taught me so much about how to love. You understand me like no one else ever has. God, please! I'm going to miss you so much."

We hugged again. "I'm going to miss you, too, Tony. You're the sweetest man I have ever known. I will always cherish what we have. We are one heartbeat. I love you so much. She gave me one last lingering kiss, stood up and said. "Goodbye, my sweet love," and then she left.

I was dumbfounded and decided to go to Gold's Gym for a light workout to take my mind off what had just happened. Kent stopped me at the front desk.

"Hey, Tony, how did it go down there in Australia?"

Hadn't he heard? I figured the entire bodybuilding world knew of my disastrous third place. While it wasn't my fault according to the judge, I felt embarrassed. I was totally crushed and I really didn't feel like re-living it with Kent. "That's it. I quit." I said. "I can't go through this anymore. I placed third. Can we talk? I trust you. You've been in my corner from the start."

"You know you can trust me, son." Kent looked perplexed. I guess he needed an explanation from me. Maybe he thought my shape was off down there, or I just wasn't trying my best. I had to tell him the truth.

"It was all a set-up. The whole show was strange. A judge pulled me aside to tell me that I'm never going to win, but I'll always place in the top five and I'll always make money."

Kent looked astounded. "I can't imagine that. I'm so sorry, kid."

"I'm sure that this has nothing to do with Arnold," I said. "He's always tried to help me. This must have come from the Federation. Someone there doesn't like me and I think I know who."

"Just remember, though, all is not lost." Said Kent.

"What do you mean?" I asked.

Kent explained, "Did you hear what you just said? The judge told you that you will always make money. You need money to live, right? No way should you quit. They are making you pay maybe because you competed in Serge Nubret's WABBA shows and the guest posing you did in Belize, but that's okay. The most important thing is you're back in. I'd continue to compete and make guest appearances. I know how competitive you are and how much you want to win, but you've got to be smart and take advantage of the situation. You should market yourself as a business."

A business? I was surprised at Kent's idea. Then he went on to advise me to compete in the mixed pairs competitions and make myself more available for modeling and acting. I told him that was a great strategy, thanked him, and went home feeling a little better about my future. Even though Sharon's departure deeply depressed me.

CHAPTER 43

I followed Kent's advice and began marketing myself, setting up guest appearances around the world and booking photos shoots with bodybuilding magazine photographers in L.A. The following year in early 1982, I received a call from IFBB Vice President and Chairman of the Pro Committee, Wayne Demilia. He said that they had almost a full lineup of competitors for the upcoming Pro World Mixed Pairs competition and that they needed one more couple to enter. He wanted to pair me up with Shelley Gruwell. I instantly accepted the offer.

Since my first exhibition with Lisa Lyon in 1979, Mixed Pairs had become a firmly established and recognized pro contest as part of many bodybuilding events. As mentioned earlier, this category had been introduced the following year in 1980. The men and women pairs competed against each other and were enthusiastically welcomed by the audiences. It had become a sensation. The upcoming event was in Las Vegas, Nevada, at the famous Caesars Palace Hotel and Casino.

My partner was a bodybuilder in her early twenties. She was the 1981 IFBB Pro World Grand Prix Champion, a gymnast, and an artist from Fresno, California. NBC Sports World Commentator, Bruce Mann, broadcast the event live from Caesars Palace Auditorium. "Ladies and gentlemen," he began, by speaking to his television audience. "Welcome to the 1982 Pro World Mixed Pairs Bodybuilding Championship. The top story of the show is that the defending pair champions Chris Dickerson and Lynn Cartwright are not entered. Leaving the title up for grabs among competitors from around the world here tonight. We also have a new entry, Tony Pearson and Shelley Gruwell. Tony is an AAU Mr. America and Pro Mr. Universe winner. And Shelley Gruwell, the 1981 Pro Grand Prix Champion."

The audience was in a frenzy with cheers and applauds. Mann was full of excitement as he spoke louder above them. "Tony is no stranger to couples posing. He's known for creating a winning formula. He was the first male bodybuilder to actually appear on stage flexing his muscles with a female. For the last couple of years though, he has been competing in Europe after receiving a life suspension from the IFBB for making a guest appearance at a non-sanctioned IFBB show. He's managed to get the suspension overturned!" Said the commentator.

The massive crowd reached a fever pitch with applauses. "We'll see if Tony and Shelley have what it takes to challenge this strong field of competitors. If you're not familiar with the criteria of judging requirements, take a look at this amazing exhibition by Tony Pearson and Lisa Lyon at the 1979 Mr. Los Angeles contest."

A huge big screen was lowered onstage and a three-minute video began to play of Lisa and me posing. As the video completes the commentator continued: "The artistry of their presentation is impeccable. What the judging criteria encompasses is symmetry, definition, body comparability, stage charisma, along with artistic merits and presentation. All these elements make it extremely difficult for a couple to achieve a winning score. Ladies and gentlemen, don't go anywhere. The stage is set, this should be a very exciting and competitive show in the finals tonight."

The emcee for the evening came onstage to welcome everyone to the finals, reminding the audience that the pre-judging had already been completed, and that out of thirteen couples there were three top winners. Shelley and I were among them. We took our place onstage to compete against Carlos Rodriguez and Melinda Pepper, and Boyer Coe and Corinne Machado-Ching. It was an all-American final in the pose down.

Mann told his viewers and the audience, with his powerful voice rising, "This is the third year of this new category. The crowd is eating it up. They're going crazy!"

The head judge speaks into the microphone. "Competitors, please spread out. Music please!" As soon as the music started, "Hot in the City," by legendary singer "Billy Idol" the head judge ordered, "Pose down!"

After we'd completed our intense three-minute pose down, the head judge called on us to stop. A few moments later he gathered the results from the other six judges and handed them to the emcee.

The emcee announced we have the results. "Ladies and gentlemen, in third place... Carlos Rodriguez and Melinda Pepper. In second place... Boyer Coe and Corinne Machado-Ching. And the winners of the 1982 IFBB, Pro World Mixed Pairs are... Tony Pearson and Shelley Gurwell!"

Later, back-stage, NBC's Bruce Mann was waiting for us. He congratulated us on our win and then he went on to say how much he liked our choice of posing music, "Chariots of Fire." "Tony, how does it feel to have won the title?"

"It's a great feeling. I'm a little overwhelmed. I love performing. Couples posing is like a dance. It allows you to express your creative side."

Mann turned to my partner. "Shelley, you're a former gymnast. Does that make it easier for you guys to create a routine?"

"No, not at all. It was very challenging. We spent hours and hours creating an original routine. It's great working with Tony because we both naturally understand the lines of the body and how to easily transition from one pose to another."

Mann noted that the Mixed Pairs category was on the verge of taking over the sport. "It had become a phenomenon around the world," he said into the camera, then turned back to us. "Are you guys going to comeback next year to defend your title?"

"Yes, definitely," I replied. "We'll continue working together to improve on our creative side of posing, and we are, for sure, looking forward to competing again next year."

"Fantastic!" Mann said, then he looked into the camera! "Ladies and gentlemen, we've undoubtedly, witnessed a masterpiece performance here this evening." He turned to us. "Once again, congratulations, Tony and Shelley, on such a magnificent win."

After thanking him, we left the stage. I felt good about the process of what it took to win the title. There was certainly a lot more work involved in creating a couple's routine compared to an individual one. But, all the while I thoroughly enjoyed having had the opportunity to show the artistic side of bodybuilding.

CHAPTER 44

About a week later I was returning home from the gym dressed in my regular gear of shorts, a tank top, and sneakers. I was about to enter my front door when two African-Americans accosted me, speaking in an urban street dialect. They were both completely unhinged and had guns. "Put your hands up!" Said gunman number one.

I obeyed, looking at the gun he was pointing at me. Then he said, "That's right, nigga, it's a gun." He motioned me inside. "Now get your ass on the floor, hands behind your back, and don't you fuckin' move."

Gunman number two closed my front door as I got onto the floor, then he went through my belongings, trashing the place. *They've sure chosen the wrong person to rob*, I thought.

"Look at this motherfucker with all of them damn muscles," said gunman number one "We got a wannabe body-builder. That's a white boy sport, nigga. Gimme all your money! Where is it?"

"I don't have any money. I swear, I don't have any money, c'mon, man." I was terrified but wondered why they'd picked me. They could see from my surroundings this was no luxury apartment.

"Gimme your fuckin' wallet. What's in your pockets?" Asked gunman number one.

I handed him my wallet and pulled out the pockets in my shorts to show they were empty. He looked through my wallet with one hand, while still pointing his gun at my head with the other, and threw the wallet on the floor when he saw there were only a few bucks in it. He picked up my Mr. America trophy that was sitting on the floor nearby.

He became enraged. "Mr. America, nigga please. Who gave you this piece of shit? You ain't nobody. You're on our turf. We own this motherfucker down here. You think you badass cause you all buffed and shit. I should go ahead on and kill this nigga!"

His hand shook as he cocked the gun. My head was down but when I heard the sound I glanced up, "No! Don't look the fuck at me, nigga."

"C'mon, no man, please!" At that moment I was sure I was going to die. "You don't have to do this, man," I said, begging him. "Please! Please!" It felt as if everything was moving in slow motion.

Gunman number two screamed at his partner, "Hey man, chill the fuck out. Don't do it, you crazy fool. You've been doing too much of that fuckin' snow, nigga. I ain't going down for no murder rap cause of your trigger-happy ass. Let's just take the shit and get the fuck out of here."

After hearing what he had said, I somehow slightly moved. Gunman number one said slowly, "Nigga, I told you not to move!"

Gunman number two told his partner he'd collected my small black and white television, the old stereo and tape player and the trophy. Which he planned to pawn. Gunman number one then gave me a strong warning, as he angrily said. "I got this for you."

That's when he took a bullet from his pocket and showed it to me then dropped it on my bed. "If you call the cops. I swear, we be back and put a cap in your head. You got dat?"

I was so petrified. "Yes, I got it, just don't kill me!" The two gunmen went running out the door with all of my measly belongings.

I stayed where I was for a few minutes trembling and sweating profusely, laying there clutching my aching ribs. The whole incident put me in a really wired place in my mind. It took me a couple of weeks to recover. But soon afterwards, I was back to feeling like my normal self.

A few months later, after all of the training I'd done helped me to recover my sanity and pushed me to win my next contest, the Men's Pro IFBB Denver Grand Prix Championship. It felt great to have won my first individual IFBB contest and to hold the trophy in my hands. Unfortunately, there hasn't been any magazine publicity from the show to date. The event was the first of many on the Grand Prix Tour that I was to compete in and I was eager to enter the next one, in Portland, Oregon.

I was backstage pumping-up a few minutes before I was supposed to appear on onstage when I turned around and saw Mr. Weider staring at me. Naturally, I greeted him. "Hi Joe, I didn't see you standing there." When he replied he sounded annoyed and antagonistic indicating that I was pumping-up extremely hard, and it seemed that I really wanted to win. I responded very calmly, "Yes Joe, I do want to win. I've been training for these shows for the past few months." Under his breath he said we'll see about that then he quickly turned and walked away with a disgusted facial expression.

I asked myself what did he mean with that remark? Was it a threat? I saw Dave Johns pumping-up nearby, an African-American competitor in the show. He was tall and clean-cut, with a pleasant personality. In his mid-30s, he was the 1977 AAU Mr. America. I asked him if he had been onstage yet?

"No, not yet. I think you're on before me. I overheard your

conversation with Joe. I can't believe he came all the way back-stage to say that to you. He seemed upset."

"I know. Nothing's changed. The drama continues," I told him.

"Hey, congratulations on your win in Denver last week."

"Thanks." I said. "I've got to keep my eye on you because I know you're right on my heels."

He smiled. "You're right. I'm working hard, my friend. Hey, Tony! You're up!"

"Thanks, bro!"

I went onstage and fought as hard as I could, but it wasn't enough. I placed second, as I stood on stage, I watched Mr. Weider so proudly shake the hand of the new Portland Grand Prix Champion, Scott Wilson. After my win the week before and to make it two in a row would be practically impossible, I thought to myself. With a heavy heart, I still refused to quit. I competed for the duration of my career of ten years knowing that my fate had been forecasted before the competitions had ever begun.

Not long after, I was asked by writer Ricky Wayne to visit the Weider headquarters to be interviewed for a *Muscle Builder and Power* magazine article. Ricky, was British, and Tri-racial, African, West Indies and Caucasian. He was a champion body-builder himself with a great muscular build. I was directed to his office and we sat and began to converse with the normal greetings. I saw he was blatantly staring at me.

I mentally checked my T-shirt and sweats. I'd put them on clean this morning. My sneakers were brand new but Ricky was looking at my face, not what I was wearing. He went quiet for a moment or two. I waited for him to speak, wondering what was going through his mind. He began by asking the routine questions and taking notes about my background but never anything about my childhood growing up. I was happy to repeat my usual answers, as I did to every writer, about St. Louis and the part George Turner played in my life.

31 years old

"Tony, you're one of Weider's top pro champions now. We can describe your humble beginnings as a 19-year old coming from St. Louis to L.A. on the Greyhound bus with $75 in your pocket, how you struggled through tremendous adversity to achieve your dream of becoming Mr. America. Let's call the article, 'Tony Pearson: Man on Fire!'"

He paused for a moment to look at his notepad. Then he continued to say, "You fought your way through the ranks, starting back when you won the L.A., and the AAU Mr. America in 1978, then winning three IFBB Pro World Mixed Pairs titles and the Men's IFBB Pro Denver Grand Prix Championship, and placed a close second at the Portland Grand Prix."

Ricky paused at making notes and stared at me again, he said, "You know, you look just like Michael Jackson!"

So that's why he'd been gazing at me with such curiosity. I'd heard that comment from a couple of people before, but coming from an important writer at the Weider headquarters, it had more credibility for me.

"Wow! That's a huge compliment. I kind of like the idea. Hmmm. The Michael Jackson of Bodybuilding!"

Ricky smiled. "It's no secret you recently had a rhinoplasty to change your nose. Did you have it done to look like Michael?"

"No, no. I didn't like the way my nose looked so I had surgery. If there's something you don't like about your appearance,

Germany, 1985

you should be able to change it. Just like we're always looking to improve our bodies, why can't we do the same with our facial features?"

"I agree, there's nothing wrong with it. Now, I know you are a huge Michael fan and you've posed to his music in the past. I'm going to include that into the article, and use your idea, the Michael Jackson with Muscles, you unquestionably dazzled the crowd with the Billie Jean routine at the Mr. Olympia in New York, and at your first Mr. Olympia with a respectable twelfth place."

"Thank you."

"So, said Ricky, closing his notebook. "I think we have enough to work with. I'm not sure when the article will run, but I'll let you know."

"Great. That's awesome. Thanks, Ricky."

This interview with Ricky was the beginning of the Michael Jackson with Muscles. To my astonishment, this would greatly increase my demand for bodybuilding special appearances at events. It would even lead to extensive national and international exposure appearing on muscle magazine covers, guest invites to several television Game, News and Sports shows, including (CBS) Card Sharks. ABC Wide World of Sports, NBC Sports World, and CFTO-TV Thrill of a Lifetime show. The change to my facial appearance had given me a very positive outlook on life, while it also built confidence.

Original Weight Pen at Muscle Beach, 1984

CHAPTER 45

After my Mixed Pairs victory with my partner Juliette Bergmann in 1986, I found enough time to make a visit home to St. Louis. George Turner invited me to make a guest appearance at the AAU Mr. St. Louis Bodybuilding Championship.

I was surprised after getting off the plane at the airport and entering the terminal to find myself surrounded by fans. Seems George had done a great publicity campaign to announce my arrival and participation in his annual event. He waded through the crowd to welcome me, while I spent time signing autographs and posing for photos. After a while, George told the fans in his charming language, "folks give the champ some fucking room," and pretty soon he led me to the exit where he had a limousine waiting. I told him I'd worked extra hard to get into my best shape for his contest.

"Shit, Tony, you didn't have to do that. I'm not worried. This is more of a homecoming." He said.

But I knew he knew I always trained hard for every event, big or small. He'd booked me into a hotel, and when we entered the lobby my sister Carolyn was standing in front of a giant-size poster showing me in a classic aesthetic pose. It was titled. "The Champ Returns Home" and gave the name, venue and date of the 1986 AAU championship.

Carolyn and I hugged. And as usual, she asked me, "What's up, little brother? Welcome home."

"Hey sis, it's so good to see you! It's great to be home." I said excitedly.

I introduced her to George and told her that I owed everything to him and would never have made it otherwise. He told me to cut it out that it was enough of this "gym talk crap." He left after telling Carolyn he'd leave tickets for her at the door.

The next morning I woke up with something difficult on my mind and I knew exactly what it was. With some down time on my hands before the evening event, I decided to beard the lion in her den. I wanted to face the fears that still persecuted me and to lay my terrible memories to rest, if that were possible. I didn't honestly have much hope of that happening, the psychological scars were too deep, but I figured it was worth a try. I went to visit my Auntie Bettie.

As I approached the house she still lived in with her daughter Alberta. Right away I began having a flashback. Remembering the painful episode on the stairs when she'd threatened me with her gun. Had Auntie Bettie mellowed out in her old age? I wasn't quite sure how she'd greet me, and I had no idea what my own reaction would be to seeing her again.

I dressed in a white loose-fitting pullover sweatshirt, blue jeans, and a pair of black dress shoes. My long curls were pulled back into a ponytail and I was now far from the skinny, poor little 14-year old who'd been forcibly removed from her home.

Fearfully, I knocked on the door. My mindset instantly reverted to feelings of terror as I heard her voice loudly call out, "Com'in!"

It was eerily quiet when I entered into the living room. I stood for a brief moment and looked around. A television sat on its stand and was turned off. Other than that the room was fairly empty. Auntie Bettie was sitting in her old recliner, the one she'd brought from the shack in Memphis.

"Hi, Auntie Bettie." I kept my voice low and I could hear the apprehension in it. "How are you?"

"I'm doin' fine." She squinted up at me, the pace of her speech slowed by time, in the country dialect I'd left behind years earlier. Shrunken by age, frail and small, she was but a mere ghost of her past self. "I cain't git aroun' like I used ta. Got a few aches an' pains but I'm hangin' in der. Seem like ol' age done gone caught up wit' me. It bin bout', oh God! Foeteen years since I seen ya last."

"Yes ma'am, Auntie. It's been a while." I replied.

"Com' over hea an' giv' yer Auntie a hug."

A hug? I went over to her. It must have been the first one I had ever given her. There was clearly no affection between us in the past. How I had longed for someone in my family to have given me a hug when I was a child. The only times she got close to me was to give me a beating. I gave her a quick hug and stepped back, trying to gather my composure. Out of the corner of my eye I glanced at a photo of myself hanging from the wall. Looked like it came from a muscle magazine as I was onstage flexing my muscles in one of my most muscular poses.

"Yer sister Carolyn brough' me dat beautifu' pictcha of ya. I jes' had ta put it on da wall. I'm so proud of ya, son. Ya done gone an' made somethin' of yerself."

"I guess I did, Auntie." I said hesitantly.

I was very surprised to see the photo up there. The walls were bare except for my image, and at that moment I realized the significance of it. For the first time in my life I felt that Auntie Bettie really cared. I assumed that deep down she did grow to love me. Tears blurred my eyes. I was choked-up for that little baby who was living on the edge of panic, and afraid he'd done something wrong to anger his Auntie. Now, as I looked at this pathetic old lady whose hopes of living a quiet life had been turned upside down by my dad and his threats of her life, I could understand some of her own fear. I could perhaps now, make some sense of how she took out her frustration and anger on me.

Auntie saw my distress as I tried to stop my tears. "No, son. Don' cry. I'm so sorry. Can ya please foegiv' me?" She began crying, too. I could see the deep remorse she was feeling. It showed in her face, in the way her head was bowed and in her tone of voice. "Yer Auntie Bettie did da best she know how ta do."

I paused as I tried to keep it together, "I know Auntie, I know. I can see clearly now. I... I forgive you." I said sadly, as I dropped my head.

Auntie wiped the tears from her eyes with a handkerchief she took from her apron pocket and changed the subject, asking me how I'd been.

Auntie Bettie (Only known picture), 1986

"I'm doing fine, Auntie. I'm always working and traveling. I'm in town this weekend making a guest appearance at a bodybuilding show for my old trainer."

"Yeah, Carolyn said ya bin liftin' dem weight an' ya won a bunch o' stuff. We see ya on TV showin' yer muscle. It so good ta see ya gain, son."

"It's nice to see you, too, Auntie. Well, I need to be going now. I have the show tonight. I've got to start preparing for a very long evening."

"I know, son. Ya go head on an' do yer work. When ya git a chance, giv' yer Auntie a call. It be real nice ta hear from ya."

"I will, Auntie, I will. You take care."

I left Auntie Bettie's house with mixed feelings. I knew I hadn't laid to rest all of my nightmares, but this was a big step forward. I never saw her again after that mournful visit or had any other contact. I believed Auntie when she said she was sorry, but the emotional damage had been done and was still following me. I went to the St. Louis Auditorium that evening in good spirits. I was glad I'd decided to visit her. It had cleared the air somewhat.

Many years later my sister Carolyn disclosed to me how difficult it was for her to witness the amount of pain and suffering Auntie Bettie experienced. After moving to a nursing home, she had contracted gangrene, Carolyn explained, that led to an amputation of one of her legs and endured several other illnesses before slowly succumbing to an excruciating death in 2001, at the age of 97.

The competition portion of the bodybuilding show had been completed. The emcee was at the podium preparing to introduce me when George rushed onto the stage and snatched the microphone out of the emcee's hand while he was in mid-sentence.

"Excuse me! I'll take that! You can leave now," George told him, then took his place at the podium, and turned to the crowd. I was kind of dumbfounded but not totally surprised. This was typical George. I held my breath, not knowing what he might say. For sure, I knew there'd be plenty of cussing.

"For those of you out there who don't know me," he said, "I'm George Turner. Now, I don't usually do this but I personally wanted to come out here to introduce our guest poser. He's from St. Louis and I trained this young man. He moved to California a few years ago. He's won a shitload of titles, including the AAU Mr. America and the Pro Mr. Universe."

A fan yelled out, "C'mon, George!"

"Hey, nut screw, I'm talking here. Put a sock in it. Now, where was I before I was so rudely interrupted? Ah, yes. As I was saying, this guy is always in top shape. You may have heard of him. He's known around the world as the Michael Jackson of Bodybuilding."

Another fan, impatient, yells, "Bring him out, George!"

"Hey, sunshine, let it rest or I'll take your ass outside and beat the living crap out of you. If I can please have your undivided attention for about two fucking minutes, but I know for the most of you that could be a real challenge. But please, stay with me here, folks. St. Louis, this man is one of our own. Do I need to say more? Hey, I want you to make some damn noise!"

The audience began to cheer but not loud enough for George's liking. "Hell a Chihuahua can make more noise than that. Make some damn noise! Folks, here he is…Tony Pearson!"

The music began. I'd chosen Michael Jackson's "Beat It" song, and I made my way onstage into the middle of the single spotlight. I hit my first pose, a double bicep shot. The crowd went wild. Everyone standing on their feet.

George was still yelling. "My dear friend," he said to the music person, "get the fuckin' lead out, would you? Blast the damn music, for God sakes. This ain't no wake, you asshole!"

The audience began chanting Tony! Tony! Tony! I went through my routine, hitting my poses aggressively, making sure that my hometown crowd got more than its money's worth. I felt great inside, accepted, welcomed, and loved. I knew my sister was sitting out there in the audience and some of my old school buddies. I didn't see her but I'd hoped that my adoptive Mom, Madir, was watching me, too.

CHAPTER 46

Before I knew it, I was back in Europe, this time staying in Marbella, a luxury resort town on the southern coast of Spain overlooking the Mediterranean Sea. I was giving exhibitions and nutrition seminars around Spain, and this particular week I was in Malaga, a coastal town to the east, just across the ocean to the south was Tangiers, Gibraltar, and the rest of North Africa.

There was something about Spain and its Moroccan influences that was like no other. I was fascinated about how different it was to other European countries I'd visited, such as France, Germany, and Belgium. Spain still seemed to be a medieval stronghold of ancient cities although its contemporary lifestyles were evident everywhere, especially in Madrid. Isolated for decades from the rest of Europe during the dictatorship of General Franco, its slower pace of life, similar to that of South America, appealed to me.

In particular, I was drawn to the traditional Spanish flamenco music and dancing that I'd read about. Brought to Spain by the Romani gypsies in the 16th century, the fiery dance form of rapidly snapping castanets and stamping feet, with the women's vividly colored costumes swirling about their bodies, was something I'd never seen before. The dances told a story, often a tragic love story, and the dancers and guitarists were always serious during their performances.

As luck would have it, who dances into my life but a beautiful flamenco dancer! Relaxing beside my hotel pool one afternoon, I noticed a young lady sunbathing on a lounge chair. She was exquisite, and her body was the most perfect, toned and buffed I had seen since coming to Spain. She wore a modest bikini, a large sunhat, and was barefoot. I had to meet her. I gathered the courage to approach and introduced myself. I had no idea if she was a foreign tourist or local.

"Excuse me. I don't mean to disturb you, but I couldn't help but notice that you're in great shape. Do you weight train?"

She sat up straighter and peered at me. "Sometimes I train with weights," she replied in English with a Spanish accent. "But I spend most of my time on the dance floor. I am a flamenco dancer."

"Wow! How long have you been dancing?"

"Twenty years. I started when I was three. It's my true passion." Her voice was sweet and her smile was beautiful as it lit up her face. She told me she performed in shows throughout Spain, and that her day job was as a secretary at a law firm in Marbella.

"You are a real artist," I said, admiring her body now that I was closer. "Please, excuse my manners. My name is Tony. What's your name?"

"I'm Corinna, Corinna Martinez. It's nice to meet you." She held out her hand and we shook. I sat on a lounge chair across from her, not exactly flexing my muscles but hoping she'd become aware I was in good shape, too. It only took a moment for her to get the picture.

"Oh! Wait a minute. You're that bodybuilder guy, Tony Pearson, *si*?"

"Yes. How did you know?"

"I've heard of you. You're the Michael Jackson of Bodybuilding. Ever since I was little I've been a huge Michael fan. My

Corinna Martinez, 1988

friends from the gym follow the sport and your name came up in the conversation."

"Your friends probably know I am giving seminars in Malaga."

"I'm not sure," she said. But they were showing me photos of you competing so I bought a muscle magazine."

"Are you from here?" I asked.

"Yes and no. I live nearby. I'm giving a dance performance at the Marbella Hotel in the Majestic Grand Ballroom tonight. I'll be the lead dancer. Do you know anything about flamenco dancing?"

"No, not much. But it sounds exciting." I said.

"It's the most passionate and deepest form of dance in the Spanish culture. You should come to the show."

"That would be great." I replied.

She got up. "I've got to go and get ready for rehearsals. The show starts at eight. Don't be late!"

That evening I sat in the center of the front row in the Grand Ballroom. The place was packed with enthusiastic patrons, most of the women dressed in glamorous gowns. I wore a black suit jacket over a white T-shirt, and black jeans. After all, I assumed this was a vacation spot, not that I had any formal clothes, anyway.

When the guitarists took their places for the performance, Corinna appeared on stage with her ensemble of dancers dressed in their colorful costumes, her long, dark brown curly hair flowing down her back. She began to sway, clicking the castanets, stamping her feet, and flashing her dark eyes. Then she went into the stirring dance. I sat transfixed.

Corinna Martinez, 1988

Towards the end of the show Corinna came to where I was sitting, took my hand, and pulled me up onto the stage. I guess involving the audience was part of the performance. She whispered softly in my ear, "Dance with me. I want to see if you've got any moves!"

I tried my best to keep up with her, but of course it was impossible. Besides, I couldn't take my eyes off of her. She was breathtaking. "Not too bad, sexy man. You're very intriguing. The show is over in thirty minutes. Wait for me in the lobby."

I returned to my seat and after the show I went out to the hotel lobby where a large crowd of fans and media waited to meet their national superstar, Corinna.

The musicians came out and began playing their guitars and singing as they strolled through the crowd. When Corinna appeared there was exuberant clapping. She posed for photos, signed autographs, and then came to my side.

"Corinna, what an incredible show! I can see why you are the best dancer in Spain," I told her. "I've never experienced anything like that before."

"Thank you. I'm glad you liked it. You're a pretty good dancer yourself, Michael Jackson. I like your style. We've got to hang out sometime."

This was an invitation that made my heart beat faster. With all the men in the country adoring her, and Spanish males were as handsome as they came, it was amazing she'd chosen me. She wrote down her phone number and I put it in my pocket. I asked if she lived with her parents, and she answered that she had her own *apartimento* down by the beach in Malaga.

With her fans still gathering around I saw she would be tied up for a while yet. "Corinna, I'm sorry, I must excuse myself. I have a very early flight tomorrow. I'll speak to you soon." We hugged and I left.

I called her as soon as I arrived to Madrid, but her answering machine came on, with the message in Spanish. I waited for the beep and then began singing a Joe Cocker's love song, "You are so beautiful to me." After completing the song. I also left her a message saying, "Hello, Corinna, this is Tony. I wanted to say hello with a song. I hope you like it. When you get a chance, please give me a call. Ciao."

I didn't have to wait long for her to return my call. I picked up the phone, hopeful. She told me that I had a beautiful voice, and the song was one of her favorites, and thought I was beautiful to her, too. She wanted to know how everything was going. I told her that I was finishing up my seminars and that I'd be back in Malaga in a couple of days, and would love to see her.

"I'd like to see you, too. Hey, I have an idea. What if I make dinner? Cooking is something I enjoy and I love making authentic Spanish dishes. I believe it's important for a man to have some homemade cooking."

"I like your idea." I said.

She gave me her address and a few days later I buzzed her apartment. She told me to take the elevator to the penthouse. She met me at her open door, dressed in a short, white tight-fitting dress. She looked absolutely stunning. I gave her a bouquet of long-stemmed red roses and kissed her on the cheek. Her apartment faced the ocean and we both watched the sun set through the floor-to-ceiling windows.

"Great place you have," I said. She replied that her mother was a realtor, and was renting it to her because her salary was way too small for her to afford such a place. The attraction between us was undeniable. After we kissed for a while, Corinna seductively removes her clothing as she continued to slowly kiss me then whispered in my ear that dinner could wait, she then led me into her bedroom and dimmed the lights. Sade's smooth romantic song, "Your Love is King" was the music on the tape player, and we lay on her bed and slowly made passionate love.

While our two-month relationship was a sheer delight to us both, reality reminded me that I still had to make a living. I was due in Nice, France, to rehearse with Carla Dunlap for the 1988 Pro World Mixed Pairs Championships. I had hoped Carla and I could create a unique routine that would give us an edge to reclaim the title, but we knew we had our work cut out for us. I broached the subject of leaving to Corinna as we sat in her living room on the sofa watching a video of her latest choreographed dance routine.

"I'll be away for four weeks, baby. I'm going to miss you so much. You know you're the joy of my life," I said as I kissed her. "The month will be a very crazy time for me and Carla. We have to develop a new routine and rehearse every day. Along with my diet and training, it'll be stressful, as always."

Corinna nestled closer in my arms. "I know you guys are going to be phenomenal!" She said. "For the last couple of months I've gotten so used to being with you, *mi amor*. I love you, Tony."

"I love you, too, baby," I replied, as we passionately kissed.

CHAPTER 47

The Acropolis Auditorium in Nice, France, was a sight to behold with its rich art French design. It seated 2,500 people and at our night event was completely filled. Jake Snow, announcer for NBC's Sports World, had flown over with a camera crew. He had a commanding voice and was broadcasting, of course, in English. Six feet tall, suntanned, and fashionably dressed in a black suit, Jake stood center stage looking into the camera.

"Welcome to the IFBB Pro World Mixed Pairs Bodybuilding Championship. Today we have an incredible line-up of competitors from around the world. The top story of our show is the return of former winners, Tony Pearson and Carla Dunlap. Tony and Carla won this show in 1984. Now, in comparison to Arnold who won seven Mr. Olympia titles, which is an unparalleled feat, Tony has previously won five consecutive mixed pairs titles with four different partners. But, he came up short last year by losing the title. Today we have a very strong field of competitors that will be trying to ensure Tony doesn't achieve this milestone of winning his sixth title. We'll see if the former champs, Tony and Carla, can regain the title for the second time. So don't go anywhere, ladies and gentlemen. You are in for a masterful show of artistic performances from some of the best pro bodybuilding athletes in the world."

The three finalist couples, including Carla, who was Ms.

Olympia, and I, were all from the U.S.A. During our posing routine, with the crowd cheering so loud Carla and I could barely hear our music. Soon after we had finished our routine and the head judge handed their results to the emcee. The emcee announced the other placings and we were the last couple standing. We had won again! We received a standing ovation and were handed our trophies. But I couldn't help to wonder why after my seventh IFBB victory that Ben and Joe Weider never managed to raise my hand during the award presentations.

As it were, the relationship never seemed to have flourished between us. Nevertheless, I'm extremely grateful to the Weider's to have had a career practicing a sport that I'm forever passionate about. Carla and I waved to the adoring crowd and then made our way backstage for media interviews.

Jake is vibrantly engaging as he spoke "Wow, Tony and Carla, you have just made history. Congratulations, Tony, how does it feel to have won your sixth Pro Mixed Pairs title?"

"There are no words to describe it. It's a blessing," I said. "I can't believe we did it. I'm just relieved that it's over!"

"What a great choice of music with Lionel Richie and Michael Jackson," Jake said. "I know the importance of choosing the right music and you guys absolutely nailed it!" He turned to Carla, "You're truly one of the best bodybuilders in the world. How does it feel winning your second Mixed Pairs title?"

Carla Dunlap, Nice, France, 1988

"After being away for four years and to be able to come back it's such a great feeling. Tony and I really had to focus on the transitional aspect of the routine to create something exceptionally different. I feel we accomplished that."

"That you did, yes indeed." Said Jake. "Thank you, Tony

and Carla, for a sensational posing performance and congratulations again on your win." We gave our many thanks for the interview.

Our schedule was hectic and I couldn't wait to get back to Corinna. But the French and other television stations kept us much longer. We finally returned to our hotel and got some sleep.

❖ ❖ ❖

My return flight to Spain was short and Corinna and I resumed our relationship. It was blissful being with her simply because she made it so easy. She was my dream come true. We fell deeper and deeper in love. Eventually, I was off to Italy for a couple weeks. But on the return flight I missed most of the wedding where Corinna was the maid of honor to her best friend. It was held in Seville, a city I hadn't visited before. The weather was absolutely prefect when I arrived. I took a cab to the famous and magnificent Grand Garden where the marriage ceremony was just ending. When it concluded I saw Corinna looking for me among the hundred or so guests. As soon as she saw me she ran across the large garden straight into my arms. We hugged and kissed like a couple of teenagers.

"I'm so sorry, baby," I said. "My flight from Rome was delayed. I tried to get here as fast as I could. The show, though, was great. They want me back next year."

"That's awesome! Oh my God, I'm so relieved that you're all right. I missed you. I love you!" She said as she passionately kissed me.

Corinna led me over to a white stone bench with a view of a clear blue ornamental pond where a group of ducks glided silently past. We sat with our arms around each other and she began telling me about Seville.

"This is the most romantic city in all of Spain. It's a city for lovers, like us." She said as she leaned in to kiss me. "It's where the flamenco dance culture started about five hundred years ago. The Moors influenced the architecture a great deal, like the Alcazar palace and other buildings. Oh! I forgot. Baby, my parents are here with me. I want them to meet you. Come, they are over there standing on the greenery."

I shook hands with Corinna's mother, Sofia, a beautiful, slender blonde lady, and Mateo, Corinna's father, who was a little overweight. They both greeted me with smiles, spoke perfect English, and said it was nice to meet me.

"Corinna speaks very highly of you," said Sofia.

"Thank you, ma'am," I replied. "She is wonderful."

"So you're Tony. We've heard so much about you, young man," said Mateo. "It's good to finally meet you. Hey, let's take a little walk."

As we strolled along the pathway that circled around the pond, Mateo told me that his daughter had spoken about me all the time, saying Tony this, Tony that, for the past five months.

"I think she has fallen madly in love with you. I haven't seen her so happy, between you and me. I want to make sure you're going to take care of our little girl. She has a really good heart and we don't want to see her get hurt. She's our only child. We love her to death, she's all we've got."

I listened closely to Mateo's remarks. I, too, was insanely in love. Corinna was the most exciting woman I'd ever met. Her beautiful personality, her laughter, and her loving ways filled my heart with unbounded happiness. She sparkled, like a superstar, which, of course, she was. I was so grateful that fate led me to her. I knew she was the perfect partner for me.

"Sir," I said, "Don't worry. I adore your daughter. She means everything to me. I love her so much. Sir, if you don't mind I would like to take this opportunity to talk to you. If I may, I would like Corinna's hand in marriage. I know we've only been together for five months but we're so compatible. We both knew from the first week that we wanted to be together forever."

I waited for his response. Was it too soon to ask for Corinna to be my wife? I hoped Mateo saw how sincere I was. Thankfully, his serious face as he listened had already broken into a smile. He clasped my hand, shook it, and hugged me.

"That's some of the best news I've had in a while. I think you are a fine young man. It would be an honor to have you as a son-in-law!"

Wow! His reaction was more than I ever expected. I thought there might have been a moment when he'd say that he and Sofia would think about it. But he came right out and said okay!

"Tony, we should have met a lot sooner, but Sofia's real estate work and my law practice keep both of us extremely busy. Tell you what, we have a home along the coast in Marbella. We need to make plans to have you over for dinner."

After I thanked him, he told me he used to work out with weights religiously and could respect the dedication I had, conceding it was very difficult to maintain a great shape like mine at my level. It was good to know that he had an understanding of my bodybuilding lifestyle and the time and effort it took to stay in shape.

CHAPTER 48

I was on the road again a month later, still in Spain but this time in Barcelona on the northeast coast, not too far from the French border. I was making a guest appearance at the Mr. Spain competition, and Corinna was with me. It gave her a chance to experience in person my life from the inside, the rigorous daily training, the new posing routine I had to create each time, and the strict diet I kept to.

Like I had always done, I was pumping-up backstage after the competition portion of the show had been completed. I heard the emcee began to introduce me. He was very lively and charismatic.

"Now, ladies and gentlemen, we have someone very special from the U.S.A. He is one of the top pros in the world. He is known as the hardest working man in bodybuilding. He really doesn't need much an introduction. Barcelona, please, let's hear it for the Michael Jackson of Bodybuilding! The one and only, Tony Pearson!"

The crowd erupted in cheers and chants as I appeared onstage, greatly surprising the onlookers by posing to George Michael's newly released hit song, "Father Figure." I began posing, going through my routine to tremendous audience reaction. When I finished, I was called to the podium. The emcee wanted a short interview.

"We thoroughly enjoyed the show," said the emcee. "It was one of the best performances we've ever seen. Thank you very much for being here."

He handed me the microphone expecting me, I guess, to say a few words of thanks to him and the audience. Which I did, but then said I wanted to invite my girlfriend, Corinna, to join me center stage. Somewhat confused, she came on and waved to the crowd who knew, of course, of her reputation as Spain's premier flamenco dancer. The audience began screaming Tony! Corinna! Tony! Corinna!

I reached behind the podium to retrieve the engagement ring I had hidden and met Corinna. I'm sure it was pretty obvious to the crowd what was going to happen with the small box in my hand. I knelt in front of her.

"Baby, you're very special to me in so many ways. You've always been there to lift me up when I am down. I am honored to have you in my life. What we have is true love. With this love, I want to cherish it for the rest of my life. I want to ask you to marry me."

"Oh, my God!" Corinna began to cry. "Yes, yes, I'll marry you, *mi corazon*. Oh my God! I love you so much!" She looked up at me with those lovely dark eyes, filling with tears, while her beautiful lips smiled with happiness.

I slipped the ring on her finger. We kissed and hugged and kissed some more, all the while hearing the audience cheering and screaming.

Corinna returned home alone as I kissed her good-bye before leaving the hotel. I could see her eyes began to tear up. I felt terrible I couldn't be with her, especially after we had just gotten engaged. But when work called I had taken an early flight the very next morning to Portugal for a couple weeks in what would be the beginning of a long extended tour.

CHAPTER 49

Juan Garcia, a friend and a bodybuilding promoter I'd met in Madrid, greeted me at the Buenos Aires international airport and took me by taxi to my hotel. He was in his late twenties, a bodybuilding champion himself. I loved his witty personality. We always had a great time together. As we drove the dozen or so miles into the city I saw how beautiful it was with its mixture of Spanish colonial, modern skyscrapers, and classic French buildings that reminded me of Paris.

After the 13-hour flight I was pretty exhausted and I was glad I had two days free before the show. I called Corinna as soon as I checked into the hotel, and we exchanged our news after expressing our love and how much we missed each other. I wished she was with me but she had dance commitments, and her job in Marbella as well.

I slept much of the next day, then met the media. The reporters were very respectful, asking if this was my first time in Argentina, and telling me I was very popular "down there."

"Everyone in Argentina follows you in the magazines, Mr. Pearson," said a reporter. "You are an inspiration to a lot of people. How many shows are on your schedule?"

I thanked him for his nice compliment, and then Juan returned to the podium to share our plan about future shows. It turned out he wasn't sure exactly, as we were waiting to hear back from other promoters. But he told the media I'd be staying in the country for the next four weeks.

Argentina, 1988

Another reporter said, "Mr. Pearson, the fans here are fanatical about body-building. We don't get professionals down here very often. Is there any advice you can give to all your young fans who wish to become champion bodybuilders someday?"

This was a question I liked answering because I'd always tried to live my life this way. "Yes. First, you must believe in yourself. Always surround yourself with positive people. There will be obstacles to overcome, but if you work hard, remain persistent and stay focused on your goals, you will succeed."

"Congratulations on your recent Mixed Pairs win," said a reporter. "Will you defend your title next year to make it your seventh, matching Arnold's seven Mr. Olympia titles?"

"Yes, thank you. I have every intention of trying to defend it. To all of my fans here, I'm looking forward to meeting each and every one of you. Thank you so much for your support."

Juan closed out the press conference after telling the press that he had hoped to see them at the show the next evening, saying it was going to be fascinating because I had choreographed a brand-new Michael Jackson routine.

The following evening the show went exceptionally well. I was surrounded by a group of fans afterwards who followed Juan and me to our car. I took photos with many of them, and I was finally was able to get into the car. Security tried their best to help us. Yet, still cheering, a large number of fans managed to push through the security and rushed our car, climbing onto the hood and banging on the windshield, attempting to get near me. It was getting a little scary, but I knew the people held only good intentions towards me. The energy and excitement was amazing.

"I've never seen anything like this," I said to Juan as the driver slowly worked his way through the crowd.

"I told you they love bodybuilding, and you, too. So, what's next after you leave Argentina?"

"A tour in Japan. Man, I just got engaged a couple of weeks ago and my fiancée is not going to be happy with me because I'm never home."

Flying to Tokyo was another very long flight. I managed to sleep on the plane and was feeling good when I arrived at the terminal. I wasn't really expecting the same reception I'd got in Buenos Aires, but to my surprise there was a sizable group of fans and news reporters waiting for me. The local promoter came up and welcomed me. I'd taken the time to learn a few words of Japanese as well as their custom of greeting people. I bowed, politely said my few complimentary sentences. He thanked me and we headed for the baggage claim. He insisted on carrying my carry-on luggage which was quite heavy. I bet my luggage weighed twice as much as he did! I told him I appreciated his polite gesture, but I could handle it.

I also expressed my surprise at the fairly large crowd that came to the airport, and he replied that there'd be about fifteen hundred more fans along with the Japanese media at the sports arena for the show. I'd put together a really special posing routine, and I was glad I'd made it as creative as possible, considering the vast interest I experienced in my very first day in Tokyo.

My exhibition tour throughout Japan finally came to a close. It was a huge sigh of relief and I was ecstatic to be going home to my baby, Corinna.

CHAPTER 50

My homecoming didn't go as expected. Despite the long, tiring flight, I was really excited to see Corinna again. It didn't bother me she wasn't at the airport to meet me. I guessed she was busy with her day job and dance rehearsals.

When I arrived to her apartment, I found her in the bedroom folding clothes.

I rushed over to her and tried to take her into my arms, but she resisted. She was cold and distant. What was this? I was confused. Had she fallen for someone else in my absence?

"Baby," I said. "I missed you so much. I'm so glad to be home. Is everything all right? I can tell you're upset. What's going on?"

She didn't reply. She went into the living room and began pacing back and forth. I followed her and asked again what was wrong?

"What I'm going to say, Tony, is the hardest thing I'll ever do."

I could see this was very serious. Whenever she was agitated she used her hands to emphasize her words, gesturing to express her feelings.

"When we first started going together I didn't realize how involved your work can be," she said, still pacing. "You were in

Portugal, Buenos Aires and Japan. For the first couple of months, it was really nice between us because we spent a lot of quality time together. I know you're at the height of your career, this is your life. Within the last nine months you've only been home for maybe a little more than three months. You're always so busy when you're on the road and with all the different time changes we never get to speak, I've been going out of my mind missing you." She wipes the tears from her eyes after she said that. I felt her pain.

Her gestures became wilder as her voice rose. "I can't continue like this. I want to be with someone that I can see every day, who has a normal job, and comes home to me in the evenings. I need someone I can make plans with for our future, like having a baby, a family. It's impossible for me to travel with you all over the world. I have a full-time job. I'm an independent woman. I can't sit here for the rest of my life waiting for you."

Her words struck like a dagger into my heart. I hated hearing what she was saying, I felt awful at this unexpected situation. I'd envisioned coming home to Corinna and enjoying our love together as before.

Still crying, she said, "It's killing me. You just don't know how much it hurts. I pray that somehow I'll be able to manage without you."

I pulled her close and kissed her. At first she gave in, then caught herself and pushed me away. I tried to find the right things to say that would make a difference. But everything she said was true.

"Baby, please, listen to me. It's not like that."

"*No me beses*," she said, telling me to stop kissing her. "I mean it, you stay over there. There's nothing you can say about what I'm telling you, because you know I'm right."

Corinna took off the engagement ring and handed it to me. I took it, feeling numb, and deeply distraught. This was one of the biggest shocks of my life. I guess, if I really thought about it, I could understand why she felt lonely and abandoned. We were so perfect for each other, I couldn't bear the thought of losing her.

"Oh my God! Corinna, baby, you're my world. I've been through so much disappointment in my life" I said. I took her by her hands, looked her straight into her eyes and passionately said, "Corinna, I've never known love like this before. I'm not sure if I can make it without you here with me. Please, don't break my heart. Everything I'm trying to achieve is for the both of us, baby. My career, is how I make a living. You can't ask me to give that up!"

With my pleading she began to tremble, and she couldn't face me. It was an agonizing moment for us both. But I could see she had made her decision. I tried one more time.

"Baby, look at me. You're my best friend. I can't afford to lose my friend. I love you so much. You know how much I care for you. Please, listen to me."

Corinna didn't respond. She led me to the door, opening it, and then she stood sideways in the doorway, arms crossed, crying, with her back leaning against the door frame. I walked over and pushed the button for the elevator. We waited in silence. I know that my sorrowful pain showed on my face. When the elevator doors opened, I couldn't believe that the music playing inside was a Reverend Al Green song, "How Can You Mend a Broken Heart?" With the tears tricking down my cheeks, I stepped inside the elevator, turned around, and pushed the Down button. Then I glanced back at Corinna for the last time just as the doors closed.

CHAPTER 51

My next Grand Prix tour began in Germany. Enzo, in his early 40s, owned the local gym where myself and my training partner Eric, were invited to train and practice my posing routine the morning of the show. I'd met Enzo on the tour and enjoyed his sense of humor, his happy-go-lucky spirit, and his many jokes. He saw life as a constant vacation and just being around him made you feel good.

I was standing in front of the mirror posing, and after about the seventh or eighth time of going through my routine hitting my marks, I said to myself, this would be my last practice run. As I went into my very last pose, the vacuum shot, pulling my stomach underneath my ribcage and then crushing down on my abdominal muscles, contracting them, all of a sudden I dropped to one knee in agony, grimacing with severe stomach pain. I wonder what had happened? My training partner, Eric, saw me from across the gym, he came running over to me. I was gasping and sweating because of whatever was causing so much pain. It was on the right side of my groin. Eric thought I should go to the hospital right way.

"No," I said. "I'm not going."

"You've got to go! Come on. We need to take you there now. I'll get the car and bring it around to the front entrance. Don't move."

If I wasn't in such unbearable pain, I'd have laughed. "Don't move?" I couldn't move.

"I've got to be onstage in three hours!" I said to Enzo, who had just arrived to help. Eric and Enzo and two other athletes helped me get into the car and we drove to the nearest hospital emergency room. I was put into a bed and shortly afterwards the doctor came. I told him where the pain was and that I felt like my whole body was on fire.

"Don't worry," said the doctor. "Let the nurse take your blood so I can check your white blood cell count. I'll be back as soon as possible."

When the doctor returned he told me I was suffering from acute appendicitis and he needed to perform surgery immediately.

"Your white blood cell count is ten thousand times higher than normal," said the doctor. "I advise you to sign these release papers," as he handed them to me. "It is absolutely necessary. Your life is at stake. We can't wait another minute. In my opinion, your body is already starting to shut down. How long have you been experiencing this pain?"

I told him I'd had the pain for about a week, but I had ignored it, thinking it was a strain from working out.

The doctor looked bemused and disturbed by my answer. "It's because you're in such great shape that you have been able to function. For a normal person, chances are they wouldn't have made it. Please, sir, sign the papers."

"I hear what you're saying doctor," I replied, "but I am not signing those papers. I have pre-judging in two hours. Don't you have some pills you can give me?" I could hardly squeeze the words out but thought some medication would take care of the complication.

"There will always be another competition," he said with a stern face. "I can't stress enough the seriousness of the matter.

We're running out of time, sir."

Eric begged me to sign the papers. "Tony, please. I think you should sign them."

His face, usually smiling, looked deadly serious. I finally got the message. Eric was trying to tell me that it really was a life-and-death situation. "Okay, I'll sign them!"

I didn't read the papers, found the line for my signature and signed. The doctor ordered the nurse to take me into the operating room at once!

As I was being wheeled out of my room, my dear friend Eric said to the doctor, "Excuse me Doctor. He's a professional bodybuilder. Please be careful with the scar."

"Don't worry, we'll do our best to make it as small as possible and as straight as we can," the doctor described.

I woke up back in my hospital bed. The doctor was standing by my side, smiling.

"Mr. Pearson, the surgery went very well. There was some infection, but I think we removed it all. We were extra careful with the scar. Once it heals you won't be able to see it. How are you feeling?"

"Thank you, doctor. I'm very sore. I can't get up to go to the bathroom. The nurses have to help me."

The doctor explained to me that was normal with major surgery, and that I'd need to stay in the hospital for a week.

One week later, in late afternoon, I was yelling frantically for the nurse. When she came running into the room I pulled back the bed covers.

"Look at my stomach!" I screamed. "I can smell my own flesh rotting! It's all different colors, blue, orange and purple. I've got a huge infection. Dear God, I'm going to die. God, please! I don't want to die today."

The expression on the nurse's face was pure horror. Then

she said she wasn't sure if there was a physician on staff. It was a Sunday and in Germany nobody worked on Sundays. She ran out saying she'd try to find a doctor as soon as she could. As I lay there, it was eerily quiet. I looked out the window at a miserable dark gloomy day. Worrisome scenarios went through my mind. If I died here, how would my family know? I was too young to die. This wasn't fair. After all my hard work overcoming my difficulties and sacrificing so much. Was I destined to die at the young age of thirty-two?

A doctor arrived, pulled back the covers, and was noticeably terrified by what he saw. He told the nurse and me he had to operate right away and sent her to get the operating room prepped. His facial expression was of great anxiety.

"Mr. Pearson, it's very risky to perform another surgery so soon. But this is urgent. We can't be sure of your chances of survival. I see from your medical chart you were worried about your scar but at this stage our only concern is to save your life."

"I'm scared! Doctor, I don't want to die."

After hours under the knife, again I awoke in my hospital room. I was still a little groggy from the anesthesia but anxious to hear what the doctor had to say when he came in. I had needles in my arms, tubes and monitors on different parts of my body and was told I had narrowly survived the surgery.

"Mr. Pearson, this was a very difficult operation. We thought we'd removed all the infection the first time, but there is no need to worry. We are certain we got rid of everything. I'm sorry, but there was nothing we could do about the scar. We need to leave the wound open at this time."

The doctor explained that the antibiotic cord deep inside the wound would be pulled out inch by inch on a daily basis. It sounded frightening to me. I could imagine the pain it was going to cause when the cord was pulled, but I took comfort in the fact that the doctor was happy with the result of the surgery. He also said I had to stay in the hospital for a while longer, at least a few weeks.

A few weeks? I knew it would drive me crazy if I had to stay here for a long period of time. I was going out of my mind as it was. I had a few friends in Germany, and I knew Enzo and Eric would stop by when they could. Maybe some of the other guys from the gym could stop by too.

It proved to be that four days of my life had already passed unknown by me because a few days after the second surgery I lapsed into a coma. As a result, I'd contracted a life-threatening bacterium. The doctor said he couldn't explain it, but that in a hospital environment there's always a chance of something like this occurring.

"Mr. Pearson, we don't know how this happened. We didn't think you'd make it, so we had to call in a priest to give you the last rites. It's a miracle that you managed to pull through. We've increased your antibiotics drastically to heal the wound."

Man, all of these happenings going on while I was near death. Last rites! I guess God was looking out for me after all because somehow I survived. The news was so disturbing I didn't know whether to cry, scream, or both. I had no idea how long it was going to take for me to resume my career. Neither did the doctor. All they could do, he said, was monitor me. A month later Eric and other friends from the gym were on one of their many visits to see me. But I wasn't in my hospital room. When they opened the window and looked out they saw me in the beautiful flower-filled garden trying to perform a forward lunge, while my hospital gown flapped around me.

"That's a true bodybuilder," said one of my friends. "It's a good sign, though. It means he's on his way back."

Eric yelled out to me, "Hey, Tony, man, are you crazy? You've got an open wound! Shouldn't you be in bed recovering?" They joined me in the garden, laughing and joking.

This was definitely the most challenging physical adversity that I'd ever endured. It took two months to return home in decent health, and a further six months to get back into my regular training schedule. Soon I was training harder than ever and my body responded amazingly fast. I was getting bigger and more shredded as each week passed, good enough so that I was invited to compete in the IFBB's European Grand Prix Tour. I had faired pretty well in my placings considering I was still on the comeback path. A couple months later I was invited to make a guest appearance at the Ms. Olympia competition in New York City. The animated emcee who introduced me announced I was their guest poser and that I'd almost died not once but twice months earlier.

"Talk about the will to live!" yelled the emcee into the microphone "As Tony is waiting back-stage, it's apparent he has achieved by far his best conditioning in years. His aesthetics is on point, along with his incredible size. Ladies and gentlemen, show some love, give it up, for the Michael Jackson of Body-building, Tony Pearson!"

The New York crowd went wild, applauding and cheer-ing. When I entered the stage I saw a massive television screen and heard the commentator say, "He certainly looks phenom-enal this evening. He looks bigger and completely ripped, not to mention his insane muscularity. With all due respect, perhaps the unintentional rest due to his major surgeries was helpful, even though he went through a very dramatic time over there in Germany. Oh my God, the audience is so loud I can hardly hear myself speak. Tony is definitely working the stage to "Michael Jackson's "Smooth Criminal." Look at that move. He's giving Michael a run for his money with his dancing. Incredible! What a show from Tony Pearson."

It was heartfelt to hear the crowd welcoming me like the old days, after everything I'd recently gone through. I was deter-mined to give my six-minute posing performance my all.

CHAPTER 52

I flew back to Spain feeling good, and felt hopeful that more offers would come in. A few months later I was right to be optimistic. At the gym one morning when I was in the middle of a squat session, the gym owner called me to the phone. I racked the weights, went over to the counter and picked up the receiver. It was Tom Platz. Tom was exceptionally passionate about bodybuilding during his lengthy career but had recently retired. He was a champion, winning the 1980 IFBB Mr. Universe, and he was also a frequent competitor at the Mr. Olympia contests were he had placed third in 1981. His nickname's was the "Golden Eagle" and the "Quadfather" for his remarkable thigh muscle development. His legs were known to be the best in the sport.

"Hello?" I said.

"Tony, it's Tom Platz."

"Tom, nice to hear a familiar voice. How are you?"

"Everything is great. Man, you're impossible to find. I had to reach out to all my contacts in Europe to find you. Haven't heard from you in quite a few years."

"I know. Wow, Tom, I've known you since '77 when we were all training like maniacs every morning. We blasted the "Rocky" theme song at Gold's Gym in Santa Monica, remember that?"

It was good to reminisce back to those good old days even just for a moment. "Ha, I do. That was the best time ever in bodybuilding. We can never get those days back. What have you been up to?"

"You know, Tom, how this sport works. Out with the old and in with the new. My career is looking a little bleak at the moment."

"Sorry to hear that. Perhaps, I have some good news. I know you still have a huge following all over the world. You're a great talent. It's time for a come-back. I'm here in New York representing a new federation that will be starting up at the beginning of next year. It's called The World Bodybuilding Federation, WBF. Vince McMahon is looking for pro talent to take part."

Excitement came over me at what Tom had said. Vince McMahon, owner and CEO of the WWF (now known as the WWE). He was famous as a wrestling promoter, businessman, and film producer.

I tuned back to Tom who said, "We're looking for guys who have an aesthetic physique and possesses a lot of stage charisma. I recommended you. You're a true performer, and that's what this federation is all about. Tony, I'm telling you, this is going to be gigantic! We're starting our own magazine and developing a Saturday morning television show on the USA Network. It's going to be called "BodyStars." You guys are going to be household names!"

I smiled at the enthusiasm in Tom's voice as he told me that the whole concept was entertainment-based. But best of all, to me, was being offered a two-year contract. Was I interested? Was I ever! Of course, in my dire difficulty the proposal couldn't have come at a better time.

The plan was for me to be in New York in a couple of weeks, along with the other bodybuilders, to launch the WBF at the Plaza Hotel. Tom asked me to come up with a character name for myself. I already had one, the Michael Jackson with Muscles. But this was like developing a superhero type of character, something that would bring out more of my creative artist side.

The Plaza Hotel lobby was bustling with people, media, and eleven former IFBB pro bodybuilding athletes, most of whom I knew. I rounded out the number as being the twelfth member of the WBF team. Tom greeted me and then took me over to meet Mr. McMahon. I shook his hand and exchanged pleasantries before he went over to talk to us altogether.

He welcomed us to the WBF team. Collectively he said we would speak in a few days to hash out some of the details concerning scheduling. And if we had any questions, that we should confer with Tom. His position with the company is Talent Coordinator. He informed us that his plate was full, and needed to excuse myself. He wished us all a good evening. Gave his thanks and left.

All of us were in the mood to celebrate our good luck and catch up with each other's news. We headed to a nearby restaurant. I was still trying to grasp the enormity of this great opportunity.

The next day I was eating lunch at the hotel bar when Tom came in and joined me. He asked if I'd thought about my character name. I told him that when I was in Germany, the gym owner was watching me practice my posing one day and he called me "Jet-Man" because of my wide lat spread pose. That's all I needed to hear, it hit me.

"Jet-Man is like having wings," I said, "and trying to take flight. Plus, I've always been a huge fan of fighter jets."

"That's a great idea! We'll develop your vignette in a fighter jet, and you exit the plane after it lands. Then we'll have you walking through a tunnel onto the stage. I love the concept. Tony Pearson, Wider than a Jet! We'll have our commercial department contact you."

I told him I'd also written my own rap for the show called "The Jet-Man Rap."

"That's awesome! We'll choreograph your routine to your music. This is what the WBF strives to be. The federation needs that unique creative edge of showmanship. That's what you bring to the table."

I was relieved, ecstatic, and especially pleased to have been recognized and chosen as one of the top twelve body-builders in the business. The WBF promised to revamp my career with this dramatic new form of competition and entertainment. We became known as the WBF BodyStars.

A few months later, in January 1991, I appeared at the sports arena where a wrestling match was about to begin. There were thirty thousand hard-core fans screaming and cheering as the announcer welcomed everyone and reminded them of a new television show to be launched, the newly-formed WBF. He also apprised them of its new magazine, Bodybuilding Lifestyles, on newsstands everywhere.

"Ladies and gentlemen, don't forget to catch the WBF BodyStars in prime time every Saturday morning on the USA Network. Twelve of the best bodybuilders on the planet will be working out and sharing nutritional information and posing tips. Check out the Wild Child, the Dark Angel, the Jet-Man, and Major Guns just to name a few. The WBF has exploded into another galaxy when it comes to serious competitive competition and sports entertainment. We have one of the WBF bodybuilding superstars here with us this evening and we'll be chatting with him right after this commercial break. Don't go anywhere!"

Onto a massive big screen positioned above the audience came an advertising commercial for beef jerky featuring The Macho Man, the nickname for wrestler Randy Savage. As soon as the commercial ended I joined the announcer at his table near the ring.

"Folks, we have here one of the World Bodybuilding Federation's personalities, superstar, Tony Pearson, the Jet-Man!"

The audience began stomping their feet and chanting Jet-Man! Jet-Man! "Thank you for having me and thanks for the love," I told the fans. "The energy in this place is insane!"

"We are just a few months away from the first ever World Bodybuilding Federation Championship," said the announcer. "How are you feeling, and will you be ready for this monumental battle against some of the best athletes the sport has to offer?"

I was quite serious when I responded, "I'm feeling great. My training is on schedule. This isn't just a competition, it's an artistic presentation. The pressure is on all the guys to be at our best. We'll show the world the true essence of the art of classic bodybuilding. I promise you," I told the crowd, "this will be all-out war to see who will capture the title. I have never been more focused and determined to achieve the best shape of my life."

"My goodness gracious, well said!" Said the announcer. "Thank you, Tony Pearson, and good luck in the show. The Jet-Man, ladies and gentlemen!" I thanked him for having me on and then waved to the thunderous applauding spectators, and left.

CHAPTER 53

T he first WBF championship was held at the Taj Mahal Hotel in Atlantic City, New Jersey, in June 1991 on Pay-Per-View. They were the three announcers sitting at a table in front of the stage. One of them was telling the capacity crowd that this was the most anticipated event of the year. And it was living up to its reputation and was an epic sensation. He really built it up as spectacular with a slightly different format from other federations contest.

There was the traditional pre-judging in the morning of the contest to determine who would make the finals, but then instead of just the top three winners brought out to perform in the evening finals, as it was normally done in other shows, all twelve of us were permitted back to perform our individual routines so that hopefully they would leave a lasting impression on the judges.

Before my entrance Announcer #2 told the audience, "Let's take a look at a short vignette of the Jet-Man, Tony Pearson." Again the audience viewed the big screen showing the vignette. When it ended, my rap song was played full-blast as I walked through the tunnel that had been set up at the back of the stage.

"Oh my God!" Said Announcer #1. "Did you see Tony come in through that tunnel? He looked like a 747 jetliner! You've heard that James Brown is the hardest working man in show business. Tony Pearson is perhaps the hardest working man in bodybuilding. He's got the charisma and entertainment value that the judges are looking for."

The three announcers began a jovial discussion as I went through my posing routine.

"You've got that right," said Announcer #2. "He wrote his own rap, and what a rap he wrote! He's got my vote."

"You said that about the last competitor!" Announcer #1 told him.

"Yeah, but I mean it this time." Replied #2

"Oh, what do we have here? Asked Announcer #3. "It's Tony Pearson's trademark vacuum pose! Where did his stomach go? That pose reminds me of Frank Zane back in the day. Tony is bringing the house down!"

"At 5'8" and 215 lbs., Tony is a fine-tuned fighting machine. He's shredded to the bone." Said Announcer #1.

"Whoa, that back of his looks like a runway at the LAX airport!" Announcer #3 told them.

"He's got the best back in the business. What a lat spread." Replied #2.

"He could rival Gary Strydom for the title. That's the kind of shape he's in. Oh, my goodness," yelled Announcer #1 into the microphone.

Despite all the admiration from the announcers and cheers from the fans, it seemed as if I was luckless again as the judges weren't on board. I didn't do better than 11th that night. I'd hoped to have placed much higher, but nonetheless, I still had a two-year contract.

The following year the WBF event was in Long Beach, California. Gary Strydom again won the title, as he had the previous year. However, it seemed that Tom Platz's publicity and promotion efforts for our team were all in vain. In early 1993, Vince McMahon called a meeting at the Titan Sports headquarters, which owned the WBF, to announce the federation would be dissolved. We were all in the boardroom to hear what Vince had to say. His remarks was very brief, thanking us all for being part of the organization but that situations had occurred that were out of his control. I took the news pretty hard.

As it turned out, I was one of the fortunate ones as I'd been asked to stay on board with the company for an extra year to represent a line of supplements, ICOPRO, created by Dr. Fred Hatfield for Vince McMahon.

In 1994, I competed in several IFBB shows, but invariably didn't place very well. With the disbanding of the WBF, I thought perhaps the writing was on the wall.

Thankfully, I was still hired for a few modeling shoots, extra parts in movies, and acting in several television shows, including an episode of "Empty Nest" (S06E15 Gesundheit). But it wasn't enough to sustain me. I decided it was time to retire from bodybuilding. Most national television news and sports programs covered my announcement. Typical was the ANBB News Sports Show: "Hello, everyone. I'm Nick Cole. This news flash just in. Remember pro bodybuilder Tony Pearson who won the AAU Mr. America back in 1978? Today, he released a statement announcing his retirement from the sport." Then he displayed a photo of me on stage with my hands raised over my head on a big screen positioned behind him as he spoke. He went on to say, "The statement reads as follows: With heartfelt gratitude, I want thank those who believed in me, inspired me, and supported me in my journey throughout my career for the last twenty years. There have been some highs and some very low points along the way but with your support I have remained steadfast in following my dream. There comes a time when you know it's time to depart and move on with your life. Today, I am announcing my retirement from bodybuilding. When I look back over the years, my hope is that I have inspired at least one person. Then my life will be complete. I want to wish everyone prosperity and good health. God bless you all. Until we meet again. Sincerely, Tony Pearson."

CHAPTER 54

After I retired I fell hard into the deepest depression ever. My weight had gone up to 240 lbs., and without the incentive to training. I'd definitely hit rock bottom. I was lost. After years of always being on the move with competitions, guest appearances and traveling, of begin in demand, and then suddenly the phone to stop ringing – it was crushing. It seemed as if my whole life had been turned upside down. My emotional confusion lasted for about a year and a half or more before I'd find meaning to all of the emptiness I was feeling and refocus on a different path. That's when I started a personal training and nutrition consulting business at Gold's Gym in Hollywood, CA.

It was slow at first but my clientele gradually increased and I began to do pretty well. Within a few months I'd mentally fought my way back to the land of the living. Among my clients were, Whoopi Goldberg's husband, Lyle Trachtenberg, Sondra Locke, Kristin Bauer Van Straten, and legendary songwriter Allan Rich.

Another client was Dr. Arnold Klein. I'd go to his home in upscale Hancock Park for training sessions in his well-outfitted home gym regularly. He was well-known as the dermatologist to the stars, including Elizabeth Taylor, Goldie Hawn, and his good friend the King of Pop, Michael Jackson. I had the great pleasure of having a phone conversation with Michael, my supreme idol. I was in shock and stoked to have spoken to my all-time favorite singer and performer.

The following year was 1997. I was tired of living in apartments and decided to buy a spacious condominium in the heart of Hollywood. At the base of the Hollywood Hills just around the corner from the Church of Scientology. It was a quiet neighborhood, better known as the actors' community. I was on the ground floor with a beautiful terrace and a white picket fence. On any given day I could walk into the middle of my small quiet street and see the Hollywood sign staring back at me at close proximity.

I missed the beach, but business was thriving and demanding. I spent all my time training and consulting. One day Fabio, the famous model who had appeared on the covers of many bestselling romance novels and had been recently voted the Sexist Man Alive, came over to me at the gym. I'd seen him there many times. He suggested we work out together, and then he invited me for dinner. He gave me an address, which I assumed was a restaurant. I said I'd like to bring my girlfriend, Madonna Grimes.

"Sure," he said. He had a very strong Italian accent that I'm sure all the ladies found sexy.

Following his directions we drove up the winding streets of Beverly Hills until, reaching the top, we found ourselves in front of a vast white mansion. This was definitely not a restaurant. In the driveway I parked alongside several luxury cars. Fabio came out to greet us as he stood in his doorway. He was dressed all in white with his chest exposed, just like you see on the book covers. Madonna and I looked at each other in awe. Fabio had made plans and we all went to a trendy sushi restaurant on the Sunset Strip. We sat outside, enjoying the perfect evening weather. During the entire meal the vibe, set by Fabio, was incredibly energetic.

He was getting ready for a world tour, no longer modeling for books but involved in acting and various sponsored projects as a spokesman. He needed to step up his training, he said, and we discussed setting up a program, but more as training partners than trainer and client. It became a great working relationship.

We challenged each other with a level of intensity that a normal person could never withstand. We trained heavy and hard, dumbbell pressing 140 lbs., doing sets of 12 repetitions then completing a set of dumbbell deadlifts using the same amount of weight and reps.

Fabio and I became good friends, meeting daily for lunch at Café Roma on the Sunset Strip. On our first visit to the restaurant we met up with one of his friends, David Geffen, the billionaire film and record producer and founder of DreamWorks, who joined us for lunch. Fabio was obviously very well connected and his famous friends often had lunch with us, including former baseball star Mike Piazza.

Fabio and his manager, 1996

One day I must have been looking downcast because Fabio, who knew me quite well, asked what was wrong.

"Madonna left me," I said. "We've broken up."

"These things happen for a reason, Tony," he said, trying to cheer me up. "You can't see it now, but you're going to be fine."

He left on his world tour and returned after a couple of months. We resumed our training and enjoyed the Hollywood's nightlife, too. It was a cool scene. The clubs were the trendiest. Hollywood is truly Tinseltown.

❖ ❖ ❖

Fabio invited me to a New Year's celebration at Hugh Hefner's mansion. It was a black tie event and I rented a tuxedo, but at this stage I could well have afforded to buy one.

We arrived at Hugh Hefner's famous Tudor castle-like estate where he lived with half a dozen stunning girlfriends, not the skinny kind of models in fashion magazines but voluptuous young women. A parking valet took our car and Fabio and I went through the paneled Gothic-style hall to the pool in the huge back garden that stretched over five acres. We passed the grotto cave with its small pool inside and went to the outdoor bar. Neither Fabio nor I drank alcohol. I ordered plain water. This evening the Hefner women were all wearing skimpy, see-through lingerie. A few were dancing around the pool. A dozen or so Playboy Bunnies served drinks and hors d'oeuvres.

The party was heating up. I recognized quite a few famous Hollywood insiders, sports stars, and business tycoons, several of whom were members of Hollywood's Gold's Gym. The music rocked in the background and everyone was in a good mood, including myself. While partiers kept coming up to Fabio to say hello, my eyes wandered to the gorgeous young lady at the pool. An attractive petite blonde, who, like the others, was wearing almost nothing. Pretty soon the ladies came over to the bar, leaving the cute blonde still swaying alone to the music. I could see that her body was beautifully sculpted. I made my way over and introduced myself.

"Hi, I'm Tony. I just want to compliment you on your dancing. I'm a bodybuilder and I appreciate women who take care of their bodies."

As soon as she told me her name was Amelia I knew she was from Down Under. Her Australian accent was charming. She said she'd been living in the States for two years and that she was a professional ballerina. To prove it she pirouetted eleven times in front of me. I was hooked. So was Amelia, as I soon found out. We were instantly attracted to each other. I fell in love with her vivacious personality and kept staring at her deep blue-green eyes, to say nothing of her stunning figure.

"I work out daily with weights," she said. "I admire bodybuilders because of the dedication it takes."

Wow! Finally, a woman who understood my lifestyle!

Then I asked a question that had been bugging me ever since we'd come up the driveway.

"Why are all the women here dressed in lingerie while the men are in tuxedos?" I *wasn't complaining*, I thought to myself, *but it was a surprise*.

"That is the requirement here," she said. "It's Mr. Hefner's house and he makes the rules."

Amelia and I danced for a while, and exchanged phone numbers. I saw Mr. Hefner standing by the pool surrounded by his six girlfriends. I excused myself to Amelia and went over to introduce myself to him. We cordially said hello to each other and then he wanted to know who I'd come with, I told him Fabio. He gave me a thumbs-up and replied, great.

I headed off to the bar where Fabio was talking to Bill Maher. Fabio introduced me to him and we shook hands. Just then Kevin Spacey came over with a beautiful young lady and stood next to me. Bill was asking Fabio to come on his television show, but Fabio politely declined. At this point I had to pinch myself. Here I was, a poor little country boy from the backwoods of Tennessee, and I was partying with all of these celebrities. Could life get any better?

A week later, after Fabio left for New York, Amelia and I began dating. We spent every waking moment together when we didn't have commitments. Our whirlwind romance was incredible. Living in Hollywood and being in love with an amazing girl was a dream come true.

But unfortunately, the dream didn't last. After about a year or so, Amelia and I drifted apart. Moreover, I was getting burned out with work, the Los Angeles traffic, and the whole frenetic atmosphere. I was exhausted. It even felt as if my health was declining, although I worked out and ate right. What could it possibly be?

CHAPTER 55

I decided to move to Las Vegas in 2001. I sold my Hollywood condo, said goodbye to everybody, and bought a new condo in Summerlin, an upscale suburb of Las Vegas. I only knew one person there, legendary pro bodybuilder Diana Dennis, whom I'd known since our competing days. She and her partner competed against me in the IFBB Pro Mixed Pairs competitions and we remained friends. There were six Gold's Gyms and I was pretty sure I could work as a trainer and consultant at one of them.

I signed up new clients and worked out daily as part of my lifestyle, just as it had always been. But I began feeling a lot of joint and muscle pain. My body experienced intense stiffness and agonizing discomfort. I pushed through it for almost two years, thinking it was normal. I wore my weight lifting belt, cinched tightly around my waist incessantly to support my aching back in an attempt to relieve the pain. I had no idea what was wrong with me. And I suffered until it became unbearable.

I went into the sports physician's office dragging my right leg, hunched over and leaning forward like an older person. The doctor was looking at my charts and at the reports from two specialists I'd recently visited. "Mr. Pearson," he said, "You are undergoing chronic joint and muscle pain all over your entire body, and you're dragging your right leg. Is that correct?"

"Yes, sir, Doctor. Every time I move I hurt. Every day it's

become a challenge just to get out of bed. I have to hold my breath. I remember the day I tried to perform a set of free squats with only the barbell, but I couldn't. The pain was too severe. I've been taking a lot of over-the-counter medication in order to function. My muscles are extremely tight; it's excruciating to stretch. I can't sit or stand for any length of time. I'm at my wit's end. Emotionally, it has taken a huge toll on me."

The doctor asked my pain level on a scale of one to ten. I told him eight and often nine. I listened carefully to his reply.

"I'm very familiar with your sport, it's year-round. I understand the goal is to achieve an extremely low-body fat condition before your competitions. On a health note, this is unnatural and could be potentially dangerous. You've had an exceedingly extensive career, putting your body through years of maintaining a low body fat content, compounded with years of heavy lifting. This can dramatically affect your muscles and joints."

The doctor went on to explain that heavy lifting breaks down the muscle fibers, therefore enhancing muscle growth, but it also produces minuscule amounts of scar tissue as well. The tissue hardens, he said. "Imagine, Mr. Pearson, over the course of twenty-five to thirty years, how much scar tissue can grow and spread throughout your body, inhibiting blood circulation to the area. As a result, the tissue becomes unpliable and hardens with the consistency relative to concrete. This leads to what you're encountering. From your x-rays you have developed an unprecedented amount of scar tissue."

This was devastating news. I sat there in such disbelief.

The doctor was still speaking and what he said next left me paralyzed with fear. "It appears over the years you have pushed your body beyond its physical capacity. In other words, you've completely destroyed yourself. There is no known treatment at this time to remove the scar tissue. Maybe deep tissue massage, physical therapy and medication can help relieve some of the pain. If there is no advanced cure available in the near future, we're confident within five to ten years, you will be permanently crippled and unable to function. From my experience the majority of professional athletes don't escape unscathed. It just comes with the territory. Also, there is a strong possibility you might require a hip replacement for your right hip in the near future."

Future? What future? I was so scared at what I was hearing I could barely breathe. I had unknowingly damaged my body. As I became teary-eyed, sitting there looking defeated, I said slowly to the doctor, "With everything I've gone through in life, all the sacrifices, my childhood, and to end up this way, how am I going to make it now?"

He looked at me then nodded sympathetically, but there was nothing he could do. He knew it and I knew it. I was done.

CHAPTER 56

Some things never change. My whole life had been centered around bodybuilding and the gym, so it was only natural for me to continue training, attending to my clientele and trying to hide how much I was suffering. I'd drastically reduced the amount of weight I used, sets and repetitions, and kept mostly to machines. But it obviously wasn't enough because one day, a few months after the doctor had diagnosed my condition, a guy who looked to be in his mid-30s approached me. I had just completed a set on the machine bench press.

"Hey, man, my name's Glenn." We shook hands and I told him my name. "I can see you're in a lot of pain." He said.

"Yeah? How can you tell?" I was sure he could hear the frustration in my voice, then he said, "It shows on your face and your body language is very telling. I think I can help you. I specialize in a unique style of treatment. Soma Flow Therapy, the art and science of structural body healing. Using what's called internal *chi* energy force. It allows me to penetrate deeper into the muscle tissue, releasing the tightness and unraveling the scar tissue layer by layer in the process. In other words, restoring the muscles back to its original blueprint."

Removing scar tissue! What? This guy can't be serious. I'd never heard of such nonsense. Two specialists had already told me that there was no cure. I adjusted my weightlifting belt a little tighter around my waist, which made me draw in a quick breath from the torment. Glenn's expression turned straight-faced when he said, "Tony, you've got that belt on so tight! You really need some help."

I told him I'd never heard of his type of work before, and that I was going to my massage therapist and seeing a chiropractor three times a week. He gave me his business card and asked me to make an appointment. I kept the card but didn't follow up on his suggestion.

A year later I was leaning against the counter at Gold's gym when Glenn came up to me and asked how it was going. Grimacing, I told him I was still hurting. Glenn's eyes seemed to have the ability to look through me.

"Just come to me once," he said, and he went off to start his workout session.

I thought about it and figured, what did I have to lose? A few days later I decided to give it a try. I'd run out of options. After taking a look at my body, front and back, he told me he could see I had damaged myself grievously. His next remarks didn't help, either.

Glenn Hall, 2018

"Your right hip is very high and your right foot seems to be permanently turned outward. Your torso is leaning forward. You're unable to stand up straight because your core muscles have been completely compromised. Your neck is twisted slightly to the right. I can see you're completely unaware of what's happening to your body. Please take off that weight lifting belt. You need to throw it out, it's nothing but a crutch. Now, take off your shoes."

I removed them. Glenn asked what was in my left shoe. I told him it was an orthotic that my chiropractor recommended for me to wear because my left leg was shorter than my right.

"Nonsense!" He said. "Throw it out. You have been mis-diagnosed, which has exacerbated the situation. I am confident I'll be able to correct most of your issues. Part of my work is to heal you physically and emotionally. I'll be teaching you to listen to your body through the mind-and-body connection."

This was the first positive opinion of my medical worries that I'd been given in two years. I'd found a spark of hope. I got onto the massage table, face down, as Glenn went to work while he explained his technique.

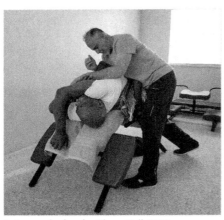

I was excited and did a little research into this new treatment that was unlike any other I'd heard of. I discovered that *chi* is the life force with which you can overcome illness, become more vibrant and enhance your mental capacity. It is found in many ancient cultures.

Being worked on by Glenn Hall, 2018

While Glenn toiled on my chest and stomach, he told me I would never be the same as when I was young but to trust him and be patient. We set up an appointment schedule and gradually, as the months went by, and as Glenn worked his expert skills, his promise was realized and the pain began to diminish.

In 2005 my stepdad Tommy Lee passed away. He and my Mom had been married for 40 years, and I knew she'd be lost without him. I flew to Memphis for the funeral. He'd been a steadfast husband to her, one of the kindest men I had ever met.

Tommy was a World War II veteran and received full military burial honors. Four soldiers in dress uniform fired their rifles in concert to give him a three-round volley salute. *Taps* was played by the bugler, to me the saddest music ever composed. It fit my mood perfectly. When it was finished, one of the soldiers presented my Mom with the American flag that had been draped over the coffin. It was a beautiful ceremony.

Later, the family and I went back to my mom's house. She was having a very difficult time, tears streaming down her face. But she assured us she was going to be fine, and that her niece, Deidra, always checked on her. I promised I'd make certain that the rest of the family would step up and be there for her as well. And I apologized that I had to be on a red-eye

Stepdad Tommy Lee Smith, circa 2002

flight back to work that same evening. I probably wouldn't make it back for her birthday, either.

"Last year when I was leaving, Mom," I said. "Tommy told me that was what he'd hoped for, to be here this year when I came home for your birthday. Your birthday is only three weeks away. I wish he'd been able to hang on long enough to celebrate it with you."

I began to tear-up as I remembered the moment.

"Don't cry, baby," she said. "It'll be all right. Tommy was 76, and he had a good life. He was so proud of you. He'd go and find every magazine you've ever been in. He'd come home and show them to me, and say, "Yeah, Tony won another one of those mixed couples things."

Knowing my Mom needed all of us in such a difficult time, I made it a point and returned home to celebrate her birthday with her and the family.

◆ ◆ ◆

In 2007, I was back at Muscle Beach. Everything looked the same. The energy and the vibe were still there. I kind of missed the workouts down there.

Thousands of people were crowding the beach and boardwalk. A podium had been set up and I was standing at it, next to the emcee.

"Ladies and gentlemen," he said, as he spoke into the microphone. "We would like to take this time to give our annual Muscle Beach Hall of Fame Award to a recipient to honor current and former champion bodybuilders in the sport. Today's award goes to one of the original pioneers of the Muscle Beach guys from the mid-70s. Thirty-one years ago, this young man made his way to the West Coast, following his dream of becoming a world

Hall of Fame Ceremony, Muscle Beach, CA, 2007

champion bodybuilder. He was discovered here by Arnold as he was working out one day, and in a couple of years he went on to win the AAU Mr. America, followed by winning Mr. World twice. He won the Pro Mr. Universe and is a six-time winner of the IFBB Pro World Mixed Pairs championship. He's the Michael Jackson of Bodybuilding! So, please give it up for the Venice Muscle Beach 2007 Hall of Fame Award. It goes to...Tony Pearson!"

I hadn't received such a great response from the crowd in years. I was honored to have been recognized. John Balik, owner of *Ironman* magazine, presented me with the award, and then I was handed the microphone. I thanked everyone and waved to

Venice Beach Hall of Fame plaque

the energetic crowd. It felt great to be back at the Weight Pen after so many years had passed. It was a very special moment.

There was an interesting occurrence that happened when I was at the gym in Las Vegas soon thereafter. As always, it was packed with members working out to resounding music. I had just completed a light set of standing barbell curls. I looked at Glenn, who was standing nearby next to a weight machine.

"Coach," I said, "is it time?"

"Is it time for a comeback?" He asked.

"Yes." I thought I knew what his answer would be, but I wasn't all that assured. I'm not sure if I even wanted an answer.

"It's time. You're ready." Glenn's smile was wide, mine not so much.

"You know, I just turned 53, I said. "And I'm twenty pounds overweight, right? I haven't been on a stage in eighteen years. I've even forgotten how to pose."

52 years old, Las Vegas, NV, 2009

Glenn said in his usual calm voice. "You're a pro. You'll figure it out. You've got to get back into the fighting mode, it's still there. It never leaves you. You just need to tap into it. Start by visualizing exactly how you want to look. That will be your mental picture. Then you will need to adjust your training accordingly, no matter what it takes to achieve your goal. Remember, it's you versus you. I can only give you advice from the sidelines." His encouraging words instantly fired me up, not from what he said but how he said it.

I told him I felt ready for the challenge and that the time had come. I had a few friends in Europe and I planned to go over there and start my training.

CHAPTER 57

Arriving in Europe, I was still fired up from the subtle speech Glenn had given me. But then it hit me as I realized just how old I was and that this wasn't like the old days. I knew this would be my toughest challenge to date. I'd began my seven-days-a-week, double-spilt training schedule. I was committed not to miss a single day. My diet couldn't get any stricter, consisting of high protein, complex carbohydrates, and vegetables. My fat consumption was one almond per day. I'd become a loner, except for conversing with a few members of the gym. I was a man on a mission. I'd never been more determined to prove to myself that I could achieve that mental picture that I'd seen when I began the program. After eighteen years though, I had no idea how my body would respond to the diet or how my physique would look. The human body composition changes every decade or so.

But I was pretty sure that my bone structure hadn't changed. Although I hadn't stopped training during all those years and probably had gained a great deal of muscle, just the *idea* of returning to the stage was terrifying.

I said to myself, *if only I could shed the twenty pounds of fat, then I'll be able to assess what direction to take in my training.* I'd alternated between gyms in Holland and Germany, and within a few taxing months I'd gotten into great shape. To keep in touch with my family and friends back in America, I posted photos of my progress on Facebook on a regular basis, showing me at the gym in numerous bodybuilding poses.

52 years old, arrival in Europe

One day Glenn called. "Hey, Tony, I've checked out your recent photos and I think you need to pull back. You've gone too far. Your body fat seems to be down to about two percent and you could be putting yourself in danger. I'd recommend adding a few fats to your diet."

Wow! I didn't expect to hear this but I was grateful for Glenn getting in touch and guiding me. I was in close contact with him and he'd never mentioned anything before. I guess after six months my body was burning a lot more than I was consuming.

"Okay, thanks, coach. I'm glad you caught that. I'm in such a mental zone. When I get so fine-tuned it's hard to evaluate myself properly. If you think I'm that low, then I will definitely increase my fats. I trust your judgment."

He suggested including a small amount of almond butter into my diet every other day. Then he gave me a motivating message.

"It's going to be alright. You're on the right track. Stay focused. Remember what I have taught you. It's all about your inner *chi*. The *chi* controls all."

"I'm with you, coach. I'll speak to you soon."

I did as Glenn proposed and adjusted my diet. The results began to show almost immediately. Man, he certainly knew his business.

♦ ♦ ♦

In 2010 I was invited to make a guest appearance in the Netherlands with one of my previous Mixed Pairs partners, Juliette Bergmann, a Dutch bodybuilding champion, sometimes referred to as the "Grecian Ideal." She was a three-time IFBB Ms. Olympia winner. This was a great opportunity to begin a comeback in Europe, to remind fans I was still around. I was also invited to make a guest appearance at FIBO Power, a huge annual bodybuilding expo in Cologne, Germany.

On the night of show, the emcee was delighted with excitement when he introduced Juliette and me to the audience.

"We have a huge surprise for you this evening! Our guest posers are from a time when aesthetic bodybuilding was the norm. These two fine athletes are known for their classic lines and their mastery of the art of posing. This lady needs no introduction. She is bodybuilding royalty, from the Netherlands, Juliette Bergmann!"

The audience went crazy standing on their feet cheering and applauding her. The emcee went on to say, "People have been asking, whatever happened to Tony Pearson? Well, he came out of retirement. He's back! And he's here tonight! He and Juliette are performing to "The Beautiful One," by the legendary singer, Prince, the same music they posed to when they won the title in 1986. Ladies and gentlemen... Tony Pearson and Juliette Bergmann!"

Rehearsing with Juliette, Middelharnis, Netherlands, 1986

Juliette and I appeared on stage to deafening applauds and

cheers. I was amazed that they had remembered me after eighteen years. I felt gleeful when they began chanting our names. Tony! Juliette! Tony! Juliette!

We finished our routine to a standing audience acclaim and applauds. I returned back to states with a new focus toward improving upon my physique and, of course, with the thought of competing again.

CHAPTER 58

I continued the training and maintained my onerous diet that had given me such great results, and in 2014 I decided to compete for the NABBA Mr. USA title. It was my first real competition since 1994 and I was now fifty-seven years of age. I was entered in both the Mr. USA Grand Masters class for those over fifty years of age and the Short Open category.

Glenn was backstage in the pump-up room where I was preparing for the finals along with the other finalist competitors. He saw I was breathing kind of hard in the middle of a set of push-ups. After finishing the set I told him that there was some tightness in my joints but I could manage it. But then I began to feel a little depressed because I felt that bodybuilding had changed so much over the years. It felt like a whole different world out there.

"We still have a little more work to do on your body," Glenn said. Then he said, "I've heard you're down on both scorecards in the Grand Masters and the Short Open class. I wouldn't worry too much. I know you've gone through this in the past." At that moment with a concerned facial expression he stared straight at me. His voice became lively like I'd never heard before as he gets into my face, saying, "C'mon, champ. You have to dig deep and pull this thing out. We've worked too hard to fade now."

He was right. I kept posing, focusing more intently as I

contracted each pose while I watched myself in the mirror. I could tell that my nerves were beginning to get the best of me. I couldn't let that happen. I turned on an internal switch in my mind and faced Glenn.

NABBA Mr. USA Grand Masters, 2014

"I came here to do a job and that's what I'm going to do! I've got to go out there and outwork them. It's going to be a real tough fight in the pose down, but I'm ready. It's time! I feel like I'm twenty-something again."

"That's the spirit!" Glenn shouted.

Glenn gave me the incentive to fight. He'd said what I needed to hear. I did one more set of body squats and another set of strong push-ups. Immediately, I was getting a crazy pump. I felt a rush as if my chest was going to explode. Then I aggressively stood up with my game face on, and said. "I'm ready, let's do this!"

"Go get'em! Champ," Glenn said spiritedly. The show was a success. I won the NABBA Grand Masters and the Short Open class title. My comeback was complete. It was such a personal triumph I couldn't wait to call my Mother and share the good news.

"Mom! Mom! I won!"

"What did you win, son?"

Celebrating with Mom, 2014

"The Mr. USA Grand Masters title."

"Oh, my Lord." She said. "Well, I'll be! You've been blessed. You sure know how to make your Mama proud."

I told her I did it for her, just for her, and that I'd be home for Thanksgiving so I could eat all the bad food I wasn't allowed to have on my strict diet. She promised to make my favorite sweet potato yams loaded with brown sugar and butter, just the way I liked them.

At sixty years of age, I made an appearance returning back to where it all began in 1976. I was invited in 2017 to appear at the Venice Muscle Beach Classic. My mixed pairs partner was Nancy Fong, a national bikini competitor, an actor, and a mom. The emcee recited my accomplishment and reminded the audience that I'd been inducted into the Muscle Beach Hall of Fame in 2007, and that my career started there thirty-five years ago. Nancy and I had chosen some of the same music as I'd used previously from the legendary singer Prince's "The Beautiful one." We received a huge welcome from the massive crowd. The two and half minute routine went very smoothly as we finished our performance. The audience loudly cheered and applauded. We raised our hands acknowledging them, and then bowed and graceful exited the stage.

Guest Posing with Nancy Fong, Venice Beach, CA, 2017

After a fun filled show I figured that would be my last stage appearance although I've persisted to train and of course, maintained a healthy diet. I originally competed at the Arnold Classic in 1990, and after twenty eight years I decided to travel back, returning to Columbus, Ohio in 2018. I thoroughly enjoyed the four-day event socializing with friends and witnessing some of the best pro athletes to grace the stage in the business.

Visiting with Arnold Schwarzenegger at the Arnold's Classic, 2018

After returning home from Columbus, I took a little excursion to Los Angeles, CA. Working out with Fabio at the Equinox gym in West Hollywood. It was great catching-up with my long time friend. We trained hard as usual and then had lunch on the Sunset Strip as we reminisced about the good old days.

With Fabio, 2018

When my sister came to visit me in Las Vegas, her first remark was, "What's-up little brother." Some things never change.

I've never forgotten what she said when I was leaving St. Louis back in 1976, "It's my job to look after you." Since I was the youngest, I guess she took that task upon herself. She always made an effort throughout the years to ensure my well-being and supported me on my journey of fulfilling a dream to

With Carolyn, Las Vegas, 2006

become a champion bodybuilder.

Sadly, we all lost George Turner in 2013, at the age of 85. I'm forever grateful to all that he had taught me about training, life and most importantly, respect for yourself and others. We miss your colorful language and your big heart. Rest in peace my friend.

My great friend Kent Kuehn passed away at the age of 83 on July 4, 2019. I will always treasure your friendship, generosity, thoughtfulness and dedication you gave to the sport. Rest in peace my iron brother.

CONTEST CAREER

1981

Canada Pro Cup – IFBB, 4th

Grand Prix Belgium – IFBB, 6th

Grand Prix Wales – IFBB, 5th

Universe – Pro – IFBB, 3rd

World Grand Prix – IFBB, 4th

World Pro Championships – IFBB, 3rd

1982

Night of Champions – IFBB, 6th

World Pro Championships – IFBB, 6th

1983

Grand Prix Las Vegas – IFBB, 6th

Grand Prix Denver – IFBB, Winner

Grand Prix Portland - IFBB, 2nd

Grand Prix England – IFBB, 4th

Grand Prix Sweden – IFBB, 6th

Grand Prix Switzerland – IFBB, 6th

World Pro Championships – IFBB, 8th

1984

Canada Pro Cup – IFBB, 3rd

Olympia – IFBB, 12th

World Grand Prix – IFBB, 3rd

1985
Night of Champions – IFBB, 9th
Olympia – IFBB, 12th

1986
Los Angeles Pro Championships – IFBB, 5th
Night of Champions – IFBB, 4th
World Pro Championships – IFBB, 9th

1987
Night of Champions – IFBB, Did not place
World Pro Championships – IFBB, 8th

1988
Grand Prix US Pro – IFBB, 6th
Niagara Falls Pro Invitational – IFBB, 5th
Night of Champions – IFBB, 8th
World Pro Championships – IFBB, 8th

1989
Grand Prix Germany – IFBB, 9th
Grand Prix Spain (2) – IFBB, 9th
Grand Prix Spain – IFBB, 9th
Grand Prix France – IFBB, 11th
Grand Prix Sweden – IFBB, 11th

1990
Arnold Classic – IFBB, 6th
Houston Pro Championships – IFBB, 6th
Ironman Pro Invitational – IFBB, 8th

1993

Chicago Pro Championships – IFBB, 13th

Night of Champions – IFBB, Did not place

Pittsburgh Pro Invitational – IFBB, 16th

1994

Ironman Invitational – IFBB, 14th San Jose -16th

EPILOGUE

For years I'd lived with a dark secret and I'd vowed to take it to my grave: never to expose my awful circumstances. But then I'd found the courage to reveal my life by writing this book. I've learned that everyone has a story to tell, but most are too ashamed and embarrassed. Writing my story was very therapeutic. It helped me to come to terms with my hidden emotional turmoil. I've found a sense of freedom, and I'm able to breathe for the first time in my life knowing that I'm no longer living a lie. I'm sharing my life's story in the hopes to inspire others to heal and to free themselves from their issues and allow them to have the trust and belief that it's okay to tell someone. Remember the phrase: "It's okay now."

It's okay now to live your truth.

It's okay now to share your story.

It's okay now to start anew.

It's okay now to be you.

You can only play with the cards you are dealt. What I have learned from my life is that despite the challenges I encountered, the past is the past. You can't change history. But you can change your perspective towards it.

THE END

Printed in Great Britain
by Amazon

38464086R00169